Goodnight,
Morning

Goodnight, Morning

JO RIPPIER

COLIN SMYTHE

Gerrards Cross 1977

First published in 1977 by Colin Smythe Ltd.
PO Box 6, Gerrards Cross, Bucks.

ISBN 0-901072-54-0

Produced in Great Britain
Set by Watford Typesetters Ltd., and printed and
bound by A. Wheaton & Co., Exeter

Contents

'Aegina' appeared first in *Die Liebschaften des Zeus,* (Nymphenburger Verlagshandlung, Munich, 1969), 'Money Matters' in *Dichter Europas erzählen Kindern,* (Gertraud Mittelhauve Verlag, Cologne, 1972).

Goodnight, Morning

Forward she went, and back; back down the corridor. It was so easy, as easy as flying. Curious, too: past lighted doorways; flash, flash, flash – she whizzed along, light-spattered, foot-light, skimming down the years, the corridor narrowing, darkening, ejecting her suddenly on to the lawn, before Miss Knightley. As then, shock stumbled her. Down went the tea-tray.

'Oh, Amy, you wicked girl!'

'Oh, oh!' grabbing the coverlet and holding it tightly, Amelia Tucker awoke, rigid with childhood fright. At first, nothing. The house grumbled and quivered as a train passed through the underground-station next door. Amy hardly noticed the trains any more, they were as much a part of her life as the rattle of a tin bowl outside the door. It was repeated.

'You're a naughty cat,' she said. 'you're a naughty cat, giving me a fright like that.' Though I can't think why he should have done, she thought, he always comes in at this time. The cat seemed hardly to touch her down-stretched fingers as it sped towards the saucer near the stove. It lapped silently, arching its great black puff-ball back.

'You're a real morning cat, you are. What can you do with a cat like that: not so much as by-your-leave, and as for saying, thank you. But then what's to be expected of a cat that came in with the milk,' she said, remembering the first morning he had pushed past her as she opened the door, had sat by the stove, waiting and looking at her. 'You don't even look any more, do you? Can't miaow either; all my other cats did. Perhaps it's my fault for calling you, 'Morning'. You're

7

certainly the quietest cat, I ever did meet. And the coolest, can't even get near enough to stroke you.' She filled the kettle, put it on the stove, took out the old brown teapot and set it on the dresser beside the red and worn-gold caddy.

She moaned slightly as she went into the bathroom cold, to wash. Her breath misted the mirror as she bent her short-sighted face forward. 'You're not very pretty, are you?' she muttered. Even when she rubbed the glass with her hand, the face she saw appeared whiter still, as if it wasn't her own, almost as if it wasn't there.

'What an old hatchet; hmph, well, I suppose it doesn't matter any more. Oh, the fish, must get the fish this morning. Early-closing day, today.'

'Not too much, now,' she said, tipping half a spoonful back, 'It's got to last the week.' She poured out the weaker cup for herself, waiting for the second to become stronger in the pot.

Up the basement stairs, slowly now, heart going faster than her feet, stop at the top to catch breath, along the passage, knock – 'once is quite enough, Amy' – enter.

'Good morning, Miss Knightley, nasty morning,' she said, putting the tray by the bed before pulling back the long grey curtains. The hand above the sheet twitched.

'Haven't said good morning since your hearing went, have you, dear. Must get that fish, shan't open your window this morning, Miss Knightley, nasty morning.'

Down the stairs again to drink her own tea at the kitchen table, knees together, back to the stove, looking at the best plates on the dresser opposite. She sat, her head trembling slightly, in the long basement kitchen. Above, the feeble light still burned – 'a forty-watt bulb will do very nicely, Amy' – and there was no window. The stove was kept burning summer and winter now, since the kitchen had become so damp. The cat slept, its plump black sides just perceptibly rising and falling.

Amelia rose from her chair, quietly because of the cat, and crept up the outside stairs to fetch the papers. Drips of black morning fog clung to the railings. On the road the traffic choked, mutely. People on their way to work stared painfully into the cold November murk. Amelia walked the few steps to the news-stand and picked up the papers.

'Terrible weather,' she said.

'Yers,' the man replied to a woman beside him. 'I reckon that'll put paid to the racing for today. Just my luck.' Amelia tucked the papers under her arm, went down the steps to the long dark downstairs kitchen to begin her morning.

'Mustn't forget the fish,' she said, later, on her way to the shops.

'What did you say?' someone asked.

'That really was the nicest dish,' his companion replied.

The fog was everywhere, thick, clammy, cold. 'Complacent! That's what that cat is; complacent,' Amelia thought. 'Never a look or a wink. Never knew a cat which couldn't miaow, either. Wonder what it does at night. Mustn't forget that fish.'

'Terrible weather,' the shop assistant said, putting Amelia's small parcel of fish on the counter as she took an order from a large-faced woman who was scratching her nose.

'My husband says the racing's bound to be cancelled, and he should know,' the woman replied. 'Ooh, what a draught. Who opened that door?'

'Eggs, I shall want eggs, perhaps there'll be some cracked ones, cheap. What funny-looking biscuits. Don't want biscuits, don't like biscuits, not those funny-looking ones, anyway. Always get lost in these places. Now, where's the tea, never can find the tea. Well, fancy that, tuppence a quarter off. Not my kind, but tuppence is tuppence. She'll never notice, never seems to notice anything these days. Tuppence off. Maybe get some better bacon, now. Fish wasn't too expensive either. That was *my* money. – "Never get anything for cats on the housekeeping, Amy, can't afford cats" – But she likes them, you know you like them, Miss Knightley. – "No, can't be bothered with cats, Amy. Things are so expensive, Amy, the roof needs doing". Now what else do I want. Ah, milk, nearly forgot Monnie's milk. Margarine; anything else? Now there was something else. Tomorrow's lunch, what was tomorrow's lunch? Chops. Yes I think chops will do. She

didn't like that sausage, but she does like a chop. Least, she
used to. Cabbage or cauliflower? Cabbage; do her good, it's
cheaper, too. How much is all that going to be . . . just got
enough; exact money.'

She laid the coins on the hard rubber counter. The girl,
dreaming, saw the money when Amelia had gone and swept
it slowly into the till.

Amelia's shoes made no sound on the pavement, the fog
swallowed the normal street sounds, or smothered them in
a mantle of grey quenching damp. People passed her by,
muffled-up, indistinct: a heavy lorry, more felt than seen,
moved just beyond view.

'Where's the tube?' a face asked and went away, staring,
before she could even open her mouth. She turned.

'First turning on the left!' whispered a voice.

'Second!' she called out.

'Why couldn't he wait a moment. Why didn't he give me
a chance to answer properly. I should know, I've lived here
long enough. I could get back home with my eyes shut. Might
just as well today, too. Just need to touch the railings . . . some
of them gone now. Best ones went in the war; lovely big ones
they were. Couldn't get my hands round them as a child.
Funny how I used to love touching them, even when I was
older. That was the day, too, when I managed to get my
hands right round; reassuring somehow. Soon be home anyway. What a day. Hardly a day at all, more like night. Glad
I got that fish. Shan't have to go out now for a couple of
days.'

Back to 124. Back indeed.

'You get off the Number 10 at Billingham Road,' her
mother had said, 'and walk till you come to 124; and watch
how you go.' It had not been difficult to find.

One-two-four; the three numbers polished above the
clenched-fist door-knocker which she had lifted so timidly
that first time. It had been more of a tap than a knock. She
had had such a fright when Miss Knightley – Miss Julia, as
she then had to address her – had wrenched open the door.

'If my father catches you playing that trick again, he'll have the police after you.' then, seeing the bag in Amelia's hand, she had stopped: 'are you the new parlour-maid? You don't look very strong. Come in.'

'124?'

'Yes, that's right, Bert. You get off the Number 10 at Billingham Road, and walk till you come to 124. And watch how you go, as my mother would say.'

'Right ho, love.'

'Amelia!' Miss Knightley always used her full name when she said nasty things. 'I don't like to think hardly of you, but we really can't have you being seen with young men on the basement stairs. This is a respectable neighbourhood. Do you understand?'

Oh, yes, she had understood all right. But she hadn't understood when Bert. . . .

'One-twenty-four? That's right isn't it, Miss Amelia Tucker? Telegram for you, Miss!'

'Regret to inform you . . .' the words were all too familiar in 1918.

One-two-four, the numbers on the front door were damp-dulled and the brass handle froze into her fingers as she turned it to enter the hall. She picked up the letters, laid them on the table without bothering to look through them, and went down the stairs to the long dark kitchen. The stove smoked into the room, adding sooty patches to the grey ceiling. 'It'll be done in the spring,' Miss Knightley had promised some years back, but the stove still smoked. Amelia went to the cupboard under the stairs, hung up her coat, put her hat on the shelf at the top, stretching up as she always had to, placed her umbrella in the corner where it slipped into the groove it had worn in the linoleum. She made her second cup of tea and sat down at the table, holding the cup between her palms. It was very quiet down here. Her quick light breath caught the steam rising from the cup in eddies. Her eyelids dropped and the cupboard at the end of the long dark room blurred.

'This'll never do,' she said suddenly. 'Must get on. Got to

get my cleaning done.' She took a biscuit, dipped it in the tea, let it crumble on her tongue.

'What would mother have said . . . ?' she thought, going back more than half a century, 'You've got teeth haven't you? Well, use them!' She hadn't any more, not her own anyway: besides she could do what she wanted now, and she'd only had one biscuit. . . .

There was the washing-up, Miss Knightley's rooms needed doing, too; oh, those stairs . . . up and down, up and down. If only she knew . . . but she did . . . not that she cared. But then, it wasn't much fun for her either, not being able to hear any more.

Somehow the work got done, even after her illness. She lay down after lunch. Late in the afternoon she set about making Miss Knightley's tea. Three rounds of bread and butter, a piece of that cake the vicar's wife had brought, the last piece. She'd sit for an hour and then go off to bed. Saved fuel anyway. It was more comfortable, too. Better get the papers for her, she liked to have the evening paper.

Amelia put her coat on again and climbed up the outside steps. The fog was blacker than ever. She picked up the paper, glanced at the headlines which she could just read in the orange neon glow.

'Terrible weather,' the man said over his shoulder away from her. Amelia read: 'No Racing today.'

'You were right,' she exclaimed.

'Just my luck,' the man said, banging his companion on the shoulder. 'Had a cert, too. This weather'll be the death of me.'

Amelia returned to the long dark kitchen to make tea.

In the sitting-room Miss Knightley was leaning forward in her chair, looking into the fire. She held a letter crumpled between her fingers. The cat sat tucked neatly on top of a large cushion on the other side of the hearth. It too stared, though Amy never knew what it was looking at. With its bushy wide-spaced ears it took on the appearance of an enormous black owl. Its eyes were round, too, like an owl's, which Amy found very strange. This time the cat seemed to be looking in her direction, although Amy couldn't be sure.

She set the tea-tray down on the small table next to Miss Knightley and laid the paper on the arm of the chair.

'Terrible weather,' Amy said. Miss Knightley stared into the dying glow of the fire. Amy stirred up the ashes, put on some pieces of coal but the fire, if anything, grew dimmer, settling quietly for the night.

'I think that's everything,' Amy said, 'You staying here, you lazy creature?' The cat continued its lengthy round-eyed gaze at the black lumps in the fading glow.

Amy left the room and went down the stairs, taking the last of the dying day with her. It seemed even darker in the kitchen, even though the daylight never entered. She sat beside the table knitting, her needles ticking like an irregular run-down clock, knitting something warm for her god-child whom she had not seen any more since the people upstairs had moved into the country. They hadn't even written at Christmas. Couldn't blame the child, she was far too young to understand and had probably forgotten her Aunty Amy.

She looked up suddenly, wondering what was different. The stove had gone out.

'Bother,' she said, 'no point in making it up now. I'll do it in the morning. Monnie won't need it and I don't feel the cold. I'll do it in the morning, tomorrow's another day. May as well go to bed.'

She stood up, put her knitting in the box on the dresser below the small wall mirror.

'Mirror, mirror on the wall, who's the fairest of them all?' she said, thinking of her mother again. She looked closer.

'Just a shadow of her former self, just a shadow,' she sighed, quoting a phrase she had seen in the paper. 'Ah, well.'

She tidied her things, washed, undressed quickly. She pulled back the counterpane and got into her narrow bed, winding the covers round her. She felt pleasantly enclosed in the folded double sheet. The door opened slowly, Monnie entered and came towards the bed to sit, staring. He opened his mouth, quite wide, but there was no sound.

'You are a funny cat, Monnie, you going to stay with me tonight?'

Amy stretched out her hand. The cat laid a paw on her bare white arm, the claws slid out, fastened, and were withdrawn. Amy felt nothing. She looked at the deep impression in the skin from which no blood came.

'All right, all right, I know you want to go out. What on earth do you do out there in the streets all night. Wouldn't you rather stay here and keep me company?'

The cat waited by the door and slipped out into the night. The thud of the bolt rang hollow in the long dark room. Amy got back into bed again, and switched off the light.

Casual Relations

She really was that sort of woman. It wasn't so much that she was bad, but that she so desperately wanted to be good. Those of you who have been children will know exactly what I mean. She wasn't even a proper aunt, either – that would at least have been some excuse. She was just a next-door neighbour. In any case 'aunt' is one of those titles affected by grown-ups when they want to ingratiate themselves with children and aunt Tabitha was no exception in this respect. At the beginning I seem to remember her mostly as a noise, and an unpleasant noise at that. My infant memory tells me no more. I came somewhat late into the world: I wasn't overdue or anything like that, but I had been preceded by so many brothers and sisters that there wasn't a great deal of room left for me and I was handed round rather like the last piece of cake on the plate which nobody quite knows what to do with. I don't wish to suggest that I was neglected or that I was unkindly treated. It was not as simple as that: I was just, well, not much bothered with. And that suited me fine. The trouble was that aunt Tabitha *wanted* to bother, and for as long as she lived next door, she did, too. Then she married; to everyone's surprise and to my own personal relief. She moved out of town and from then on was only an occasional nuisance. When she came though, there were presents, annoying thank-you-very-much presents. I couldn't say that these rare visits were enough to sour my view of the world, although the Christmas I am going to describe easily might have done.

15

Two weeks before the day, my mother became ill. It was unbelievable, how could she do such a thing, why couldn't she wait for a more convenient time. All these thoughts rushed through my mind. I didn't of course realise that it could be serious: till then illness for me had meant lying enjoyably in bed since I never had more than an occasional cold. Christmas was home time, family time, warm, cosy, noisy. Everybody was there, the real aunts, uncles, all the family; lots of cousins to play and fight with. I was spoiled, ruined, as my mother put it, from morning to bad-tempered night.

But not this Christmas.

'Now, Johnny, I want you to be a very good boy!' my mother said. I knew this voice: it meant that something unpleasant was coming. 'Your aunt Tabitha has very kindly said you can spend Christmas with her. Now isn't that nice of her.'

'No!' I said, although it was quite hopeless. If aunt Tabitha wanted me and the grown-ups had agreed, there was nothing I could do about it.

'Now, we'll tell Father Christmas where you're staying and he won't lose anything on the way, I promise. And when you come back, if you've been a good boy, I'll make you some toffee-apples. Would you like that?'

'No!' I said, but not quite so emphatically.

And that was that.

The next afternoon I was put on the bus and left to wonder what I should do with myself during the long days ahead. Our house was always full, always noisy. The cool cold quiet of aunt Tabitha's made me shiver slightly whenever I entered it, and I felt eyes watching me all the time. The country bus stopped outside the gate. I gave one loud bang and two more timid knocks on the front door. Clip-clop, clip-clop, went my aunt's shoes on the stone hall floor. Clip-clop, clip-clop, chasing away good spirits.

'Hello auntie,' I said.

'Ah there you are, Jonathan;' she bent her woodpecker face down: peck, peck, two dry little kisses rattled round the draughty hall. 'Oh, look, your scarf is all undone, your coat's muddy, have you got your bag, you look rather pale, are you all right, how's your mother and DO wipe your feet.' A series of questions which left me speechless and more than a little intimidated. Of course I now realise that aunt Tabitha didn't mean any harm, and actually was herself rather apprehensive.

'Come in and have some tea,' she added. 'The kettle's boiling.' I brightened at this: I had forgotten aunt Tabitha's teas. We went into the small drawing-room at the back of the house. Even today I can see that tea-table set for three, with its crackling stiff-starched white table cloth. On it there were currant scones, drop-scones, apple plate-cake, rock cakes, lemon-curd tarts, fruit-cake, my own special favourite, egg custard, white and brown bread and damson jam – all home-made. On Sunday evenings, fruit salad and cream. At least aunt Tabitha never minded if I ate as much as I wanted.

'But,' I asked, 'where is uncle Tom?'

'Uncle Thomas,' she corrected me in that high-piched chisel of a voice of hers. 'I don't approve of abbreviations!'

'I do,' said uncle Tom . . . later, when we two were sitting together.

'Now, don't you take any notice of her, she can't help it, she's had a hard life!'

'Uncle Thomas,' my aunt continued, 'has been having his afternoon nap. I'll go and wake him. It's time for his tea, too.'

Uncle came in, with care, leaning on his stick. He always smiled; in spite of the pain.

'Hello, boy,' he said, 'nice to see you!'

Tea was a quiet meal, as indeed were all occasions when the three of us were together. Uncle sat nearest the fire, eating slowly, little, and with difficulty. I watched, horrified and tense each time he lifted the trembling cup to his lips, not understanding his struggle. Occasionally he would glance round at me, and if my aunt was not looking, would wink, his special uncle Tom wink. It was a wink for all time. It said, I know you don't want to be here, but don't mind too much, we'll manage somehow, we'll have a chat later, it's all right, don't you worry. A slow laborious wink which my aunt never noticed and which she wouldn't have understood if she had. After tea aunt looked meaningfully at the clock on the mantlepiece.

'It's time for a boy of nine to be in bed' she said.

'But he hasn't been to see me yet.' protested uncle Tom before I could open my mouth.

'It's nearly time for a sixty-year-old uncle to be in bed too,' aunt replied.

'Are you sixty, uncle Tom?' I gasped.

'Uncle Thomas!' aunt cut in.

'I am indeed, my boy,' he answered. 'I'll see you in the morning. You mustn't argue with your aunt, she knows best.'

But bed in this house was not like bed at home. There I had my own little snug next to my parents' room and always in the comforting background grown-ups at their evening noise.

But for all the strangeness of the house I fell asleep almost immediately, to wake some hours later, all my senses alert, waiting, ah waiting. But for what? An old house always moves at night. Tick tock, tick tock, tick t-tock went the old grandfather clock on the landing. I shut my eyes tighter: I was suddenly very small. I froze to the rasp and shriek of an owl, followed by the echoing silence of the wind round the house. A tile shifted, a cat mewled unmelodiously, the night was all around me.

And then I slept again.

'How's your tree?' uncle asked, some days later.

'Fine, thank you, uncle Tom.'

'I'm glad, boy, I'm glad. It's not much fun for you here with us old folks.'

'I like being with you,' I replied, rubbing the backs of my knees against the cold leather of the chair into which I had clambered.

'You mustn't mind your aunt. She's had a hard life, she's always compensating,' he said. I didn't know what he meant and didn't like to ask. He went on to tell me about his first wife, which didn't interest me, and then about the mountains, which did.

The fells had been the first and lasting love in his life and

he had walked them for over fifty years. I have never seen
them but if I do, I am sure I shall hear uncle Tom's nutmeg-
grating voice in my ears and see his robin-redbreast cheeks
and slow wondering blue eyes before me. I have been on those
hills so often in my imagination that I think I should be a
little frightened of the reality. I shouldn't like to lose uncle
Tom.

'Tell me about the tree, Johnny,' he said. But I couldn't.
My tree was at the bottom of the garden, an ivy-covered oak.
Inside its leafy fork I could look out into a new world. From
this point only the day before, as Robin Hood, I had trans-
fixed my unwitting aunt to the kitchen door with an arrow
from my trusty long-bow. The vicar passing along the road on
the other side of the hedge had been consumed in a gush of
boiling pitch. Then in the middle of a fight with three huge
savages whom I was fending off with my sword while hanging
by one arm from a gigantic creeper, my heroic efforts were
interrupted. . . .

'Jonathan, come in this instant, your lunch is getting cold!'
Back into the house crept, once more, unwillingly, a little
boy. Inside the house, except in uncle's study, I felt uncomfortable. Everything was so clean and neat. In the mornings
the shining breakfast table would hiss: 'Hands off my
polish!' the carpet in the lounge muttered: 'Careful,
Johnny!' as I walked over it. 'Ow, Ow!' the stairs would cry
as I kicked my way up them. And the round copper kettle
in the corner of the hall said: 'We don't like little boys,
Johnny, we don't like little boys.' But aunt did try. My
slippers did scratch the floors, I did fall rather than come
down the stairs, the carpets were never straight while I was
there; and each time I realised too late. Often aunt Tabitha
said nothing. Her mouth would open, to shut suddenly with
a mousetrap snap, and that was all. Then for ten minutes at
least I crept round on tiptoe, hardly daring to look at the
furniture whose long-suffering and disapproving gaze I felt
concentrated on my diminishing person.

But Christmas was coming, even at aunt Tabitha's, and
some few slight concessions to the season of merriment and

joy were made. We had a Christmas tree; outside the house of course where it would not make a mess, and judiciously placed so that the neighbours, with whom I was not allowed to play, would be able to see it. Oh, and holly, cut into tight little sprigs, wiped over with a damp rag – careful, Jonathan – was put into small silver vessels and round the downstairs rooms. There was even a chaste little bunch of mistletoe attached to a warming-pan on the drawing-room wall.

And then, I suppose, there was Christmas. But the funny thing is that I cannot remember it at all. No doubt I continued to spend the mornings with my uncle and the afternoons in the garden. I do know that there was no snow that Christmas: it was mild and wet. And nothing else. But isn't that like most childhood memories. They start with a toffee-apple, and, as in this case, they will probably end with a toffee-apple which I received because uncle Tom, bless his heart, told my mother that I had been a good boy.

Happy Christmas, Mr Rouge

Mr Rouge was not a nice man: indeed he admitted it himself sometimes when asked to do a favour or for something from the factory stores which he either didn't have or didn't want to hand out: 'No', he would say, scratching a chin whose smoothness depended on how near the day happened to be to when it had its weekly shave: 'It's no good coming to me with your daft requests. I've had to look after myself all my life, and that's as much as I can manage. I don't bother other people and I don't want them bothering me: so be off with you.' he would bark and shuffle back into his store, although shuffle is not the right word. Shuffling implies rubbing the sole along the floor, thus wearing it away. Rouge's walk was more like a silent dead-march, his feet seemed to remain just above the ground without actually touching it.

For all his air of advanced decrepitude, old Rosy – a nickname which was not so much a bad pun as a description of the colour his face never showed – still managed to move so quickly that he was generally out of earshot before outraged feelings could be translated into speech. And of course people never asked a favour twice.

His unfriendly manner was known, and feared, in the factory. From his very first day at work – at the time the firm itself had only just opened – complaints had been made about his ill-temper. Nothing, not even threats of dismissal from the managing director, had had the slightest effect. Rouge had listened to warnings, nodded slightly, then turned and walked away without saying a word. Even the owner of the firm felt somewhat intimidated by this solitary man. Since Rouge did his work well, was punctual, never ill, and refused to join a union, the owner had finally decided to accept him on his own terms.

It was 5.25 on Christmas Eve. Rouge locked up the stores, went over to the porter's lodge after putting on his crumpled old mac and flat cap, which he wore so low over his brow that the slightest movement of his head removed from view anyone he did not wish to speak to or greet. This included most people, and particularly members of his own family who still tried to remain on good terms with him on account of the money he was reputed to have.

He chuckled to himself at the thought. He had been as rude as he liked to all of them, insulting them individually and severally, but, with the tenacity born of avarice, they had suffered his insults, consoling themselves with the thought that he was bound to die some day. But he had lived so long that some of his heirs had rather lost heart, and begun to wonder if he were not blessed, or cursed, with an ability to stay alive when others passed away. 'I'll outlive 'em all', said Rouge to himself, and chuckled again. 'You all right, Mr Rouge?' asked the porter, who, never having seen him laugh before, wondered what the curious noise was.

'Course, I'm all right', Rouge growled, and, turning up the collar of his mac, went into the street.

'Miserable old beggar', the porter muttered to himself.

It was a bitter cold evening, fog was thickening, adding its own kind of nastiness to the unattractive surroundings of the factory. The other men rushed past, hurrying home. In the poor light of the lane leading up to the high street, they looked like so many tadpoles, bobbing and sliding in the swirls of mist.

As usual, Rouge had left his shopping till the last minute. As he approached the brightly-lit line of stores, he lifted his head slightly to scrutinise what was still unsold. He entered a butcher's shop.

'I wondered if we should see you again this year', the butcher said. 'You were nearly too late'.

'I don't like buying when all the women are around',
Rouge answered.

'You mean you don't like paying the proper price', the
butcher replied, 'so you wait till the end when we have to
sell off cheap'.

'You're all robbers, and you know it'.

'I've got just the thing for you', the butcher said, ignoring
Rouge's last remark. 'How about this beautiful 20 lb turkey.
You can have it for five quid. I'll tell you what, since you're
an old customer of mine, I'll let you have it for £4.10.'

'Now what on earth should I do with 20 lbs of turkey!'
Rouge answered.

'Well, you could invite all your relations to Christmas
dinner.'

'Hmph! Why should I want to invite my relations I
should like to know. Rotten money-grubbing lot they are.'

'It *is* Christmas, you know.'

'Bah', Rouge exploded, casting his eyes along the white
marble slabs, till they rested on the carcass of a small chicken.
'What's that over there?'

'Now you wouldn't be wanting that now would you, Mr
Rouge? Why, it only weighs two pounds.'

'How much', asked Mr Rouge.

'Well, it may be small, but it's very tender.'

'How much?' repeated Rouge, not to be sidetracked.

'A pound.'

'I'll give you 40p. You'll not sell it now.'

'I don't know how I'd live if I had customers like you every
day.'

'It's better than nothing, and you know it.'

'Let's say 75p, that's a 25% reduction.'

'40p it is, or nothing', said Rouge turning towards the door.

'All right then; as it's Christmas,' the butcher answered.

'Damn fool,' Rouge said to himself in the street as he
slipped the small bird into his pocket. He bought some
sprouts for 5p. Special offer – the woman said, and, after
rummaging around in an odd lot of oranges, found three
which still looked edible, haggled over the price with the

shop-keeper before finally beating her down, and then set off for home; his Christmas shopping done.

He turned down a quiet street lined with chestnut trees. The orange neon lights gleamed wetly through the fog, throwing the houses and other objects into relief. A few last chestnut leaves fell limply, turning slowly on their way to the ground. It was very quiet and his feet sank silently into the soaked leaves. The fog clung to his face and clothes, adding smaller drops to the one which hung almost permanently from his cornice of a nose. He pad, pad, padded along, until he reached a street of stunted, smoke-blackened houses originally built for an adjoining factory in the 19th century. He stopped in front of one of these, which, like its neighbours faced on to the street. Unlike its neighbours, the step was black and filthy instead of being white-scrubbed or red-leaded, and the brass foxhead knocker had turned a greeny-grey. The paint on the door, or such as remained, hung in mottled flakes from all parts of it. Rouge entered the house and switched on the light in the sitting room, into which the front door opened. A smell of must, bacon fat and damp hung about it, though Rouge would have been the last to notice this. The shadeless bulb cast its crude light round the room. Two dirty plates and a mug stood on the table. These Rouge picked up and took through to the kitchen where he washed them under the cold tap, unsuccessfully trying to clean the grease from the plates. He lit the paraffin heater, keeping his cap and coat on, then looked in the letter-box. The day on which his bank statement arrived was the climax of each month. There it lay in its long, wide, brown envelope; it was an event only equalled by the arrival of a letter from his stock-broker. To see those short, neat rows of figures stimulated his mind in a way no letter or turn of phrase ever could have done. On returning from work he would sit and gaze at this typewritten confirmation of his wealth. To read S. C. Rouge Esq., at the head of the page gave him a thrill which never lost its immediacy. He would spend hours with the statement clutched in his hand, the figures multiplying in his mind as he worked out possible ways of increasing his capital. In the twenty years since he had inherited his wife's money, he had developed a sense of timing on the markets which never ceased to amaze his stockbroker. Rouge was fascinated by the movement of money: his eyes would sometimes wander caressingly across the financial page of a newspaper, registering and loving the words on which they lighted: scrip, bull, bear, preference, debenture, rights, contango, take-over, all of them expressions which he fully understood and which had become a part of his secret self. For a man who never spent without snarling over the last halfpenny, he was bold when it came to investing. Like Midas, all he touched turned to gold, admittedly gold which never actually passed into his hands. But it was there, waiting only for his word, so that it would be poured, thousands upon thousands of pounds into his lap. Somehow he had never really wanted to see it there.

Underneath the bank statement lay another envelope. He noted with pleasure that the stamp had remained unfranked, and before opening the letter he managed to remove it. It was a Christmas card from his nephew, on which was written 'With love to Uncle Stan'.

'Bah,' he said for a second time, 'I know what they're after, but they'll not get it.'

He rose from the ancient armchair whose shattered upholstery was hidden under a faded brown blanket. He put the letters on the ledge beside the range which had not been used for many years. A dim remembrance of cakes, bread and other dishes which had been made there, may have flitted through Rouge's mind as he hesitated, ever so slightly, before ripping up the card and throwing it into the grate. The room still bore some evidence of a woman's presence. There was some silver behind the dirty glass of the sideboard, although it was tarnished almost beyond recognition. The filthy curtains had obviously once been attractive and matched the carpet, which gave a clear indication of where Rouge normally walked to his chair.

Feeling hungry, Rouge made himself supper: bread, cheese, and a cup of water. Then, removing some of his outer

garments, he went to bed to watch TV. It was more comfortable than his chair, and had the additional advantage that he
could turn off the paraffin heater. He switched on the TV and
reached down for a bottle of beer which somebody had left
lying near his stores in the morning. The television set had
not been one of his better purchases. It had been cheap
enough, but was sensitive, both to passing traffic and the
weather. Wind, for example, made viewing impossible –
perhaps partly on account of the aerial which he had fixed
somewhat insecurely to his chimney-pot.

It was cold when he awoke the next morning. There was
frost on the window-panes. Even his false teeth, which he
kept under the pillow at night, seemed to have been almost
frozen together as he popped them back into his mouth. It
was past nine o'clock as he rose unwillingly from his bed,
washed perfunctorily, and put off shaving until the next day.

At about eleven o'clock he began to prepare his Christmas
lunch. This was one of the few occasions of the year when he
ate meat. It always infuriated him to see the amount of
money his relations spent on food, and it confirmed his ideas
on how unsuited they were to looking after anything he
might have left them.

He looked through the bag of potatoes and peeled two.
These he put into a saucepan and took out the sprouts to
clean them. He went on cleaning them for some time, until
finally nothing remained to clean. He realised that the
woman in the shop had not been such a fool after all.

After this set-back, he turned his attentions to the chicken,
which, for its size, appeared to have very large bones. Never-
theless, it looked tender, and so he decided to fry it. Apart
from anything else, it would be the cheapest way of cooking
the bird. He had just switched on the gas under the frying-
pan when he became aware of noise in front of the house. As
he listened, his front door was knocked on, while a group of
carol-singers performed 'The first Noel': neither very well,
nor for very long. As usual on such occasions, Rouge ignored
the knock and went on with his preparations. The door was
struck – not so lightly this time – Rouge stood still so that

they should think him out. He heard someone pressing the bell and smiled to himself, because it hadn't worked for years.

'The first Noel' was followed by 'God Rest Ye merry Gentlemen', and a thunderous attack on the door.

'Come on out, you mean old shark. We know you're in. We shan't go till we've got something.'

'I'll give you something all right, you cheeky young swine!' shouted Rouge, rushing forward and opening the door.

For the next ten minutes, the street was treated to a noisy altercation which may have been lacking in Christmas spirit but it was certainly something the street enjoyed, particularly when Rouge was at the centre of it. Rouge was infuriated most of all to discover among the group the nephew who only the day before had sent his 'love'. He was just shouting at his nephew when his arm was taken by one of the others, who said to him: 'Have you been cooking, Rosy, 'cos I think there is something burning!'

Smoke from the kitchen was now coming through the open front door. The chicken!

Rouge cut his finger struggling with a window which had not been opened in years. After he had cleared up the mess, he realised to his extreme annoyance that he would have to go out for a meal.

At 12.30 precisely, he left the house and made his way to the pub on the corner.

'Well, well, this is a surprise,' the landlord said, when he came over to serve Rouge. 'What'll you have?'

'Half of bitter and a pork pie,' muttered Rouge.

'Go on, make it a pint, you look as if you need it,' the man answered.

'Half a pint, I said,' replied Rouge.

'There you are, sir,' the landlord said, as he brought pie and beer and put them down in front of Rouge.

'Happy Christmas, Mr Rouge.'

'Bah!' said Rouge for the third time in 24 hours.

Money Matters

'I'm bored. . . . I'm bored. . . . I'm bored, 'Peter said, letting himself fall forward into the armchair. He knelt, cheek against the cushion, his hands sliding down the tight sides of the chair. Down they went, until they could go no further. His finger-tips touched something hard. He strained to get his fingers round it. Ah, he'd got it. Out it came: a two-shilling piece. Two whole shillings – all for him. He held the coin in his hand, looked at it. A brand new one, too; not a speck on it, not shiny, just clean and silver.

'Mummeee!' He shouted. 'Look what I've got.'

'Yes, Peter what have you got?'

'I've found a two-shilling piece down the armchair and findings are keepings.'

'Well, isn't that nice.'

'I want to spend it, Mummy.'

'I'm sure you do. Knowing you, I suppose you'll want to be off immediately, won't you. All right, off you go.'

Peter rushed out into the street, stopped. What should he do, what was he going to buy? I'm not going to spend it all in one go, he thought. This time, I'm going to think about it, plan it. It's going to be an adventure. Two whole shillings. He held the coin in his hand.

I know, I'll go into the park for a while. The sun's shining, and anyway, I've got all the afternoon.

He walked along the street, the heel and toe-tips of his shoes going clickety-click, two-shilling piece, clickety-click, two-shilling piece. The whole square seemed to pick up the

29

rhythm, right to the tops of the high buildings all round: clickety-click, two-shilling piece, clickety-click, two-shilling piece.

He stepped off the kerb to cross the road. The main entrance to the park was directly opposite.

'Hey! What do you think you're doing?' somebody shouted. 'Why don't you look where you're going?'

Peter jumped, turned round. A car had stopped right behind him.

'Didn't you see me?' Peter said, 'I haven't got eyes in the back of my head, you know.'

'You! . . .' the man in the car drove off without finishing what he wanted to say.

Once in the park Peter walked across the grass. There weren't many people about. He sat down in a deck-chair, started to think of things to buy. He looked round at the pigeons on the grass, smiling at the way they walked along; left, right, left, right, their fat bodies swaying from side to side as they went along.

'That'll be three pence for the chair, young man.' The park attendant said.

'I'll tell you what,' said Peter. 'You can have the chair for nothing. I'll make you a present of it.'

He stood up, walked off quickly.

'Hey, you young monkey,' the man shouted, 'you come here!'

Peter was off like the wind.

Two whole shillings. Outside the park again. He slowed down to think, put the coin into his other hand. It felt very warm.

He walked on slowly, thinking, thinking. He almost walked into a man in front of him, who was going even slower than he was. Peter stood still. What a funny-looking man, Peter thought. The man's legs were very bowed, inside the widest trousers Peter had ever seen. They flapped at every step. Left, right, left, right, the man's short body swayed from side to side as he went along. Peter found himself imitating the way the man walked. The man turned round.

'What do you think you're doing?' he said.

'I'm pretending to be a pigeon,' Peter replied.

'Are you now,' the man said, 'that's interesting.'

'Have you got eyes in the back of your head?' Peter asked, 'How did you see me?'

'There's eyes everywhere.'

'Are there?' Peter said.

'Oh, yes,' the man went on, 'an artist needs eyes.'

'Are you an artist?'

'Well, look,' the man said. Peter looked. On the pavement, hanging from the park railings too, were a number of paintings and drawings.

'I've just come back from lunch,' the man said, 'artists need to eat.'

'So do other people,' said Peter.

'There's no justice,' the man said. 'Take the Prime Minister.'

'I don't quite understand,' Peter answered.

'No, you wouldn't,' the man replied, 'you're too young.'

'I'm not that young,' Peter answered. 'Can I have a look at your pictures?'

'Have a look if you've the eyes to see,' the man said. 'Nobody sees things the way I do, but then, I'm an artist. I mostly do portraits. I've done the Prime Minister, for example. That's him,' he said, pointing.

'Do you know him?' Peter asked.

'I don't need to know him. One look's enough. They're all the same, these people. All those ministers, the lot of them. No good, I tell you. No good at all. But you'd better leave me now, I've got to concentrate. This is the time of day I do my thinking. It's not easy being an artist, you know.'

He sat down on a small folding seat, leant back against the railings. His eyes closed, he appeared to drop off to sleep almost immediately. Peter was puzzled. It seemed an odd way to do one's thinking. He stared at the man, at the pictures on the pavement, up at the others on the railings, back at the sleeping man. The man wasn't very old; in his sleep he was so still. As he slept, he seemed to be folding himself up, fading away. The man's cap lay on the ground. Inside it was a penny, with a foreign coin beside it.

Peter suddenly bent down, dropped the two-shilling piece into the man's cap. He turned away, to run, run, run, all the way home.

Aegina

Dear Philip,

After you have read this letter I want you to destroy it, and, should we meet on some occasion in the future, don't ever refer to it. But I have just got to tell somebody what I have gone through. I cannot live alone with it any longer. God knows, I am not very strong but the last months would have shattered someone with the constitution of an ox. I feel as if my whole personality has been taken out piece by piece, examined and thrown away, leaving just a physical presence behind.

I am writing to you for a number of reasons: you do after all know me well and you are a person who is able to keep secrets. You may even want to write. Don't! Just putting pen to paper is already helping me, although in talking to you I put myself into your hands. You live a long way away and we are unlikely to see each other for years. By then the immediacy of this experience will have passed – I hope – and so there will be no embarrassment or distress on either side.

Of course you still haven't the faintest idea what I am talking about. I have never liked talking about myself and hate being forced to face facts. I thought I had even managed to stop thinking about myself.

But let me start at the beginning. Just after we met last autumn I set off on my research trip. I am very sorry that I have not written all these months, since I know you wanted to hear about what I was doing. You may find this hard to believe, but even at the very start I was unable to

33   ·

communicate with anyone outside the valley, for reasons which remain incomprehensible to me. Now that I have left, it seems as if my mind is attempting to close the time-gap created by those months. While I was there I found it increasingly difficult to think back to the outside world, and now I am away from it, it becomes more and more of a struggle to make my mind return to this subject, in spite of the melancholy and depression which are a direct result of it. It is curious: I can at the moment almost see my mind visually, as little streamers of tissue stretching out to link up and close for ever this episode in my life. In fact I find more and more that I consider myself as a being apart, that I no longer belong to the body and personality I once inhabited. As a scientist I am intrigued: as a human being, I am frightened. To give you an example of what I was just saying; when I was in the valley, I could not for the life of me, remember how it was I first learned of its existence. Yet now, writing to you, it comes back instantly. For it was in your house that I happened to open one of your magazines at a page on which there was an article about the valley. At the time I had been looking for an area which had remained untouched by modern agricultural methods, so that I could carry out some comparative studies on insect life in limestone regions. And, as further investigation showed, this was the perfect location. As I write these lines I am taken back in time to that warm afternoon in May, the first really fine day of the year. I sat down on the chair facing the open windows in your lounge and looked down your garden across that quiet Oxfordshire valley – I still cannot understand how you could bear to sell that lovely house and go abroad again – and I was relieved when I saw that I should not even have to travel too far, and also, much more important, that the language spoken there was one in which I had some fluency. So, in a roundabout way, you are responsible for what happened; but you mustn't think that I blame you in any way. Further reading and investigation proved the correctness of my first impressions and in November of last year I set off just for a few weeks to have a first look around.

To my dying day I shall never forget how the valley looked
that morning. I had been driving hard for three days, and,
as I arrived in the area late in the evening, I decided not
to go on that night but to stay in a village on the other side
of the mountains. As it turned out, this was a sensible decision
since the roads, which had become worse and worse, were
simply dreadful over the mountain. The wine I had in the
evening probably caused me to oversleep and it was nearly
ten o'clock before I left the little guest house and drove
slowly up the road which was really no more than a rough
track.

Up and up I drove, avoiding ruts and boulders, some of
which were quite large enough to have put the car out of
action for good. It took some time to reach the top; the
clouds became thicker all the way up. I drove slowly down
the other side, using the gears as an additional brake until
I was clear of the cloud. One moment I was surrounded by
swirling cloud, and the next I was in sunshine. I stopped
and gazed down, switching off the engine as I did so. There
was a slight suspicion of wind at this height: down in the
valley nothing moved. Nothing, that is, except for the coils
of autumn mist unravelling on the sides of the valley. It
might have been smoke, but the smoke from the chimneys
in the tiny hamlet below went straight up. There was not
a sound; not the bark of a dog, not the crow of a cock;
nothing, just the gentle push of wind against my cheek at
the open window. From this altitude I could follow the
river's course from one end of the valley to the other. All
along its length, smaller channels led off in a series of loops
which looked too regular to be natural. I sat there for quite
fifteen minutes listening to the wind. It looked like a toy
island wrapped in cotton-wool.

I drove on down to the village. Actually there were only
twenty houses and the number of people living there
amounted to a hundred or so. Just away from the houses
on a slight elevation stood the ruins of what once must have
been a fine house. I was told that it had belonged to a local
aristocratic family and had been burned down at the end of

the war. Apart from this there was nothing to suggest that anything had changed in the valley for centuries. I am not going to attempt to describe things in detail. You know I am not much good at it, but I'd like you to try and imagine the scene for yourself.

Of course my appearance on the mountain road had been immediately noticed and there was quite a crowd, consisting mostly of children, awaiting my arrival. Children are always curious, but on this occasion I had the feeling that they looked at me as if I was some sort of bizarre object, solid enough, but completely beyond what they would normally expect to see, and thus not quite real. This must sound crazy to you, because although the valley is off the beaten track, it is by no means completely cut off from civilisation. There are plenty of visitors in the summer, too, who come for the fishing, or just to walk. I was the first stranger to come during the autumn and I suppose they found that a little odd.

I had an introduction to the water-bailiff and was taken to his house. It seemed to be full of young girls. One of them took me through the house to the back. I ought to have mentioned that this was the last house in the village and behind it the slope led straight up the mountain. Of course I had read all about it, but it still came as something of a shock to see the spring. Certainly, 'spring' seems an odd word to use in this context, for it was a pool fifty yards long and about twenty wide; from this, enough water flowed to form the river. As so often happens in limestone areas, it trickles away to nothing at the end of the valley, to reappear again many miles to the south.

As I approached the pool, I banged my leg painfully against a trestle on which a large black metal tank rested. 'He's not here', the girl cried, 'he'll be down at the spawning beds. It's not far. Can we take the car?' she asked shyly. We drove through the hamlet and out along the bumpy track through the meadows, until we came to a bridge over one of the feeder-streams. In the shallows I saw more large trout than I had ever seen in my life before. It was an amazing sight. Since the water was so clear, the fish seemed to be floating on air above the white pebbles, until in a sudden flurry they sent the water flying.

A little way along the stream were three people, one of them in the water. My attention was attracted from the first to the man in the water, a giant of a fellow, over six and a half feet in height. He was bent almost double to take out fish, stripping them of their spawn into containers on the bank. However it wasn't this which so fascinated me, but the way he did his work – so much so that it was some moments before I tried to catch the attention of the others there. Large people are often clumsy, but this man was a marvel of physical coordination. His ability to take the fish from the water, strip them of their spawn and return them was done with such rhythm and smoothness that his huge hands appeared to be breathing life into those invisible specks of creation.

You must forgive my mentioning these seeming irrelevancies but I do want you to have some idea of the surroundings, and particularly of this man. You will thus perhaps appreciate better what happened later.

The giant straightened up, groaning slightly as he did so. His eyes did not change expression when they met mine, for he was totally absorbed. Even when he became aware of my presence, his gaze was more inward than outward. Spaosu, the bailiff and fishery-manager, shook me warmly by the hand and introduced me to the third person, his daughter, Gina. She stood up and regarded me with that open, unashamed curiosity one often encounters in children. In an adult it is singularly embarrassing, at least to somebody like me. She did not speak and immediately sank back to her original sitting position on a wooden stump. Up till that moment I had not been able to see her face since her long hair had completely covered her features. She too was very tall, though perfectly proportioned, and, as I later learned, only nineteen. It is absolutely no use my trying to describe her. You can never describe somebody you love – or hate. You think you can, because an image pursues you constantly, relentlessly.

If you try to turn this into words, the individual features dissolve and change almost kaleidoscopically.

The first time I hardly even saw her. Her eyes stabbed into me and all I felt for the moment was the pain. I remained standing there, looking at her for seconds after she had turned her attention elsewhere. The giant remained where he was in the water, and went back to his work again. Spaosu apologised for not having met me when I arrived and invited me to visit his house that evening.

I stayed at the house of a widow in a room above the stable, although animals were no longer kept there. I arranged to take the room again on my return the next summer. I intended to remain for several months in order to complete my studies of the aquatic insect life in the valley. During this first visit I rambled along the river and the many small streams which had been made to flow round the meadows. The channels had been so constructed that they could be opened in places to irrigate the fields.

Oh, I almost forgot to mention one other person who later was to have a major, if not the major, part to play in what happened: Rhea, Spaosu's wife. It was easy to see to which side of the family the daughter owed her appearance. Physically, Gina was magnificent: of her other qualities, I shall speak later.

Spaosu told me that Rhea had never really forgiven him for taking her away from the city. Her feeling of superiority to the women of the hamlet had not made life easier for either of them. As the years passed she had become withdrawn, brooding on what might have been, and, according to Spaosu, rather letting things slide. The children, never having been checked or properly taught, had run wild. Spaosu himself was far too good-natured to assert his authority, and was now more interested in the welfare of his fishery than in the fate of his children – particularly since both his sons had been killed in the war. Gina, who often went with him while he was working, was the only one for whom he seemed to have any great regard. But I am forgetting the giant. Nobody knew what his real name was. He had been left there by refugees after the war and had grown up in the village. The community was so small and remote that it was rather like a large family. Sonnio, that's the name which had been given to the giant, had been more or less adopted by the village. Spaosu was very good to the boy when he discovered his love of the river. As a child he would play contentedly on the bank all day, touching the water with a kind of childish reverence, and, as he grew older, assimilating all its ways and wiles.

He knew where the big trout lay, where pike were likely to be found, when the eels ran; the man's mind was the dictionary of the river. Open it at the right place and there was the answer to any question. Of course it was not quite as simple as that, for he did not find it easy to put into words the knowledge he had acquired. He had hated formal school and had played truant as often as he was able. He combined the knowledge of a man with the mind of a child, but for me he was both guide and teacher.

Since Spaosu rarely walked far it was Sonnio who most often accompanied me. But the older man was often able to help me since he could look back on nearly fifty years of work at the fishery. His reputation was such that even when the present regime came to power he was allowed to remain at his post although he had been working for and had been on good terms with the old landowners.

My few days soon passed and I was often at their house. Rhea was polite, but never did more than courtesy to a stranger demanded after she discovered the purpose of my visit. She hated the river with a steady undiminishing passion. Concern for the health of the river had kept her husband in the valley all his life and she knew he would never leave it. Sonnio was the only one who could wring a smile from Rhea. Not that he ever spoke much. Away from the river, his personality changed. He stooped, shambled, and was unsure of himself in company. The children would have made fun of him openly – they often did behind his back – had they dared. One of my lasting memories of Sonnio is of him walking away from me on the last evening. It was cold and he was wearing an ancient black coat which had originally been made for a man much smaller. His great hands hung down inches below the end of the sleeves, the long fingers stretching and curling as if he had no control over them.

As for Gina, she never made the slightest attempt to notice me: my greetings were ignored. In any case she came and went just as the whim took her. The family seemed used to this.

As you know, I returned to the valley in April. During the day I would go out alone, or with Sonnio. I generally took with me bread, cheese and local red wine for my lunch, eating something more substantial in the evening, cooked by the widow. Why do I mention these things? Perhaps you will think my mind is going. Maybe it is: but you must try and see the valley and my daily existence. Since my work progressed well, it would have been reasonable to assume that I was, yes, happy. The weather could not have been pleasanter, the sun becoming hotter with each successive day. The lack of rain did not matter. The sluices on the channels were opened to flood the meadows, the water eventually finding its way back into the river.

Sonnio was somehow different. It was not that he was unfriendly or anything like that. He had become more inhibited, more uncertain of himself. He would mutter to himself and clench those fists of his till the bones crackled. Once beside the river though, he became his old self again. He talked quietly, gently, struggling to tell me what I wished to know. His eyes were never still. He had a knack of looking along the river and immediately noticing anything unusual; a movement, a ripple on the water, a stunted fish, or one which had not recovered from spawning. These fish often kept close to the bank out of the current. I have seen him take these trout with his bare hands, almost charming them out of the water. When he wanted to, he seemed somehow to be able to fade into and become part of his surroundings. Sonnio always carried a spear with him, the wooden shaft ending in a long, brightly-polished barbed tip. He told me that he had practised since youth and, as he often demonstrated, he had attained a deadly accuracy. Sometimes he would swing his huge body up into a riverside tree and crawl out along a branch. From this vantage point he would look into the clear green water below. Once or twice I clambered up beside him and from there he showed me where a pike had hidden itself so that it was invisible from the bank. He then stepped down again, quietly approached the spot and hurled the spear into the river. I never saw him miss.

Sonnio was not the only person who had changed in those few months. Spaosu and Rhea now treated him coldly. He was not invited into the house any more. And Gina? She laughed and mocked at Sonnio whenever she saw him. More than once I saw her flaunting herself in front of him when she thought nobody could see. In her eyes I was nobody, so I suppose she thought my seeing this did not matter. And yet you know, I had the uneasy feeling that she was trying to goad Sonnio into becoming jealous of me, but he was too involved in his own misery to react to such subtleties. As the weeks went by I became more and more aware of the strain under which he was living. Although his eyes were normally curiously bereft of expression, to me, watching him so closely, it was obvious that the poor fellow was half-crazed by his love for Gina. Those who love, I suppose, always see these signs.

There was one place along the river-bank to which I often went. I had boards out in the centre of the stream, under which insects laid their eggs. I took these out regularly for examination. It was also a good place to take fish when I needed to. I made a point of studying the stomachs of trout which either I or Sonnio caught. A punt was kept here, so that I could cross the river if necessary. Often I worked there for hours at a time, sitting on an old rotten stump and using a box as table. In this shady spot behind the bushes I was invisible to anyone on the opposite bank. After I had been coming here for a time Gina suddenly appeared one evening and swam in the ice-cold water not fifteen yards away from me. Philip, I tell you, that girl's body was so beautiful. And she knew it. She held me there, an unwilling observer. Unwilling . . . no, if I am honest, I could not say that. What really upset me more than anything else was the slow realisation that she was revelling in the situation of having a secret admirer.

What followed was worse. One night in the last week of May I awakened suddenly. A candle was burning on the bedside table. In front of it and facing me stood Gina. When she saw that I was awake, she took off the coat she had been wearing. Under it she had only a thin night-dress. She looked at me as she had done that first day, twisting the knives in the wound. She bent forward, her eyes still holding mine.

'You're a man aren't you?' she hissed.

Although I was too overcome to reply, I must have nodded.

'Then prove it.' she said.

She let her nightdress slip to the ground, and remained standing where she was so that I could see her before snuffing the candle and getting into the bed.

Philip, that Gina wasn't a woman, she was a witch, and what's more, I think she hated men. She took me. I cannot describe it otherwise; afterwards tossing me aside, humiliated, emptied, shrivelled. When she had finished with me, she rose from the bed and left without a word. I lay motionless, hardly breathing, mentally and physically petrified. I must have fallen asleep eventually because the widow had to knock for some moments in the morning before I answered. I forced myself to get up, and tried to continue with my work. I must have done so, although I now have no clear recollection of the days that followed. I was glad to return to my seat on the river bank where I could sit alone. Gina did not come back. I assumed that she had finished her game with me.

The weather was superb and the whole valley was a mass of lush green and flowers. The birds sang from morning to night. I am not a very romantic person at the best of times, but even in this state of suspended shock, I felt the surge of generation going on all around me. During the week after Gina had come to my room I hardly saw Sonnio – for which, as you can well imagine, I was not sorry. When I did, he was always busy – furiously busy – it seemed to me.

I was sitting in my usual place one evening at about five

o'clock. The atmosphere was heavy, the heat oppressive, and a storm was rumbling behind the hills. The hatch of Mayfly was late – no doubt a result of the heatwave – and I had a feeling that the storm might bring about this annual miracle. It is a sight which always amazes me and I wished to see it on a river which I now knew to be free of any kind of pollution. Sonnio was standing on the other side of the river, his spear held ready. He had obviously seen a pike in the weed and was waiting for it to move. The willows, swaying slightly, cast a pattern of shadows across his bare shoulders and chest. It was very still, apart from the occasional sound of distant thunder. No fish were rising and even the birds had been silenced by the heat.

Suddenly there was a splash in front of Sonnio. I looked up; he looked up, uncomprehendingly. A hot puff of wind ruffled the surface of the water. Gina was just behind Sonnio. She had a willow branch in her right hand, pressed against the top of her bathing costume. She threw it over his head into the water, in a cruel mime of his spear-throwing, and laughed at him. He sprang at her. Normally she would have been too quick for him, but not on this occasion. Physically they were a good match, and she fought hard. But this time Sonnio was not cowed. He took such a grasp on her as made her gasp and hurled her to the ground.

Large single drops of rain started to fall. While those two, locked at first in battle and then in the act of love, did what they had to on the other side, the Mayfly came out all along the river. The smooth surface was shattered as trout surged, plunged, in their attempts to take hatching or landing insects.

The air became white as myriads of insects emerged for their brief nuptial flight. It was like a snowstorm except that the snow, instead of coming down, rose, and then danced, high above the river. The air was so thick with insects that the two figures on the opposite bank became blurred and indistinct. Seagulls, swallows and swifts dived and screamed as they caught the hapless insects. Then, as the rain came down in torrents, the hatch ceased as suddenly as it had begun. The clouds hanging heavy over the mountains brought dusk with them; lightning flickered on the wet gleaming bodies of the lovers. Yes, lovers. I began to understand certain things at this moment. Some people might have called what had happened, rape. But of whom?

I was no longer alone. Spaosu was standing a little to my right, bent forward slightly as he peered across the river. He was no more than six or seven yards from me. How long he had been there I do not know. As I looked at his face, I realised slowly that it was not so much anger that I could read there, but something else. Suddenly he clambered into the punt, almost overturning it in his frenzy. He paddled across the river, shouting wildly as he did so. Sonnio heard him, sat up, looking round to make out where the sounds came from. When he saw Spaosu, he sprang to his feet and snatched up his spear.

'Get back!' he roared, 'she's mine!' Gina lay where she was and did not move.

'She's not!' screamed Spaosu. 'I'll kill you!'

Sonnio did not answer. His spear flashed in the lightning and I heard it strike. The old man remained seated at the back of the punt for a moment. He tried to rise to his feet, shuddered horribly, and then fell, lying grotesquely across the punt. I could now see that the spear had passed through his leg, impaling him to the boat which, having lost its momentum, slowly swung out into the stream.

Gina got up and would have run forward. Sonnio stopped her. 'He's dead: let him go!' He released her arm, turned, strode away while Gina sank to the ground, where she lay motionless.

I rose from my seat and walked away, through the rain. Hours later I found myself in the village again. I went straight to bed. When I awoke late the next morning, it was still raining. The puddles in the single street grew larger and larger. Down the mountain, most of which was now hidden in cloud, water was tumbling. From hour to hour, trickles grew into torrents: in the meadows, where the hay was ripening, small lakes formed. From the widow I learned that Spaosu had been found and carried to the house. When

Gina did not come back, people had gone to look for her. She had been lying unconscious beside the river and was now in a high fever. Of Sonnio, nothing was known. It cannot have been difficult for Rhea to guess the reason for her husband's fatal heart attack. Apparently she had said nothing but had picked him up and taken him to her room. Late that night she had been seen to go out in the rain.

I felt weak and remained in bed all day, sleeping fitfully and waking occasionally from bad dreams, although I no longer know what I dreamt.

The rain stopped during the night. When I looked out of my window in the morning I could see people standing beside the river, pointing and gesticulating. I dressed and went down to see what it was all about.

As I approached the group, I could see what they were looking at. Fish. Dead and dying fish. Everywhere one looked were the grey-white bellies of dead fish, bobbing slightly in the slow flow of the waters. The seagulls were back. Again they were diving and searching as they picked up fish from the surface of the water. There was nothing I could do. I returned to my room and sat there waiting, thinking. Later that day, I was roused from my thoughts by the sound of breaking glass. Below my window, a dead seagull lay on the ground. Other gulls, flying above the houses, were doing strange things. As I watched, one dived, or rather fell, into the water, flapped once or twice, and was still. Another crashed into the wall of a neighbouring house. I drank heavily that afternoon.

When I awoke the following morning, the hamlet seemed unusually quiet. I missed the sound of children, of dogs barking, of chickens. From my window I looked out again across the valley. The early morning mists were lifting and I could see that the floods had receded somewhat. I was surprised that my breakfast had not been brought up, for the widow was normally very punctual. I found her sitting in the kitchen. She had just heard the news.

Sonnio had returned the evening before. He had walked into Spaosu's house and had gone straight upstairs to Rhea's room. She wasn't there. He found her standing beside Gina's bed. According to the widow, he had picked Rhea up and hurled her through the widow. She was killed instantly. He had walked out of the house again and into the hills.

Gina died the same day.

There was nothing I or anybody else could do until the floods subsided. While waiting I sat in my room, or walked by myself round the marooned village. Animals and chickens died suddenly and violently. Nobody was drinking the water any more. People stayed in their houses, waiting. It took a week before the road was clear. Each day I could walk a little further, although it became more and more frightening to do so. There was such silence. The only sound was the sound of one's feet, sinking into the muddy ooze. Not a cricket chirped, the birds had left, the vegetation was dying. And the smell of those fish rotting in the sun; shall I ever lose my remembrance of that?

On my last morning in that dreadful place, my wanderings took me to the spring. It was then that I noticed the black metal tank against which I had stumbled shortly atfer my arrival. It lay on its side beside the water. Spaosu had once mentioned to me the weed-killer he had bought some years previously, and which it had been so difficult to transport to the village. God only knows what terrible chemical changes had taken place in its composition since then. But how had the contents of that tank got into the spring?

Suddenly I remembered Rhea's walk in the night. She had always hated the river. . . .

Sage and Onion

'I don't want a goose,' she said, 'I like turkey. We've always had turkey and there's nothing wrong with turkey. Is there?' she said, turning to the visitor.

'You're barmy,' she continued, 'and at your age, too. Do you know, he dreams about them, tosses about in bed, wakes me up with his noise. Geese!' she said, 'I'll give you geese!'

'You and your nonsense. I tell you it's not natural. And furthermore who's going to pluck it, I should like to know. Not me, I can tell you that straight away. Filthy mucky things. Just think what they've been feeding on. Ugh! It's enough to make you sick. What's more, they're as tough as old boots. And talking of boots, what about yours. All over my clean floor. Oh, look at him. Did you ever see anything like it? John James Jolly, cat-lover and goose-chaser! Why don't you shoot a few of the cats. That'd be more to the point. The place is crawling with them as it is. Can't you leave that ginger creature alone for a minute and listen to what I'm saying. Yes, me! It's your wife. I'm talking to you.'

Jolly's long fingers dug into the cat's fur. He stroked the cat in long regular movements. The cat was stretched along his knee, exercising its claws in the rough material of his breeches.

'Hey, John James, do you think I'm talking to the kitchen stove?' She banged the milk bottle on the table so that drops splashed on to its worn surface. Jolly pushed his brown tweed cap back and scratched his forehead. Above the eyebrows the skin was suddenly white, his straight hair, still thick, the colour of rain-beaten straw.

'Can't you take that thing off? Frightened you'll catch cold or something? How did I ever come to marry such a soppy creature? All he ever does when he comes in is grab that cat. . . . Another cup of tea?' she asked the visitor. 'And what are cats, anyway, nasty spiteful creatures. They only want what they can get out of you. The rest of the time you're dirt under their feet. The cheek of it. I do all the work, feed'em, put'em out at night, queue up for tit-bits for them, get the milk – you should see our milk bill – and what happens? His lordship comes home, and the cats are all over him. There's gratitude for you. I've no patience with them. Now I suppose I can go and pack some food so you can get out. Well at least that'll give me a chance to clean up again. And next time, boots at the back door – please. Ah, what's the use. I mean, just look at it, sitting in front of the fire with half a ploughed field on his boots. Must have been born in a ditch.

'You've chosen the wrong time to come and see him, I'm afraid. He's goose-mad. It happens every year, you'll not get any sense out of him.' Jolly bent his head over the cat, smiled.

'Did you say you'd have some more tea?' Mrs Jolly asked the visitor. Jolly gently lifted the cat off his knees, put it down. He stood up, walked towards the door.

'And,' Mrs Jolly continued, 'You should take a look in the bedroom. You've never seen anything like it in all your life. Shot, gunpowder, cartridges, all over the place. I'm not allowed to touch anything. Wouldn't want to, either, I can tell you. Might do myself an injury – not that he'd care – he's going to blow the house to smithereens one of these fine days. Aren't many wives'd put up with your kind of nonsense, I can tell you. Now what on earth are you standing there for. For goodness sake stop dithering and get yourself ready. But you're not going into the bedroom in those boots! I'll have your sandwiches ready when you come down. I know you, you'll be fiddling about for hours. Now get on with you!'

Jolly switched off the engine of his motorbike, sat looking down across the partly-flooded valley. The air was heavy with damp, the wind freshening although it was not strong enough to fill the ears. The hot metal under him made noises as it contracted; tall dead grasses at the side of the road rustled against the wires. The light was going and the clouds appeared to be coming lower.

Jolly sat motionless for some minutes, watching, listening. Down below, the upper parts of hedges made patterns in the water: small islands showed where the level of the ground rose. Jolly felt in his pocket for a handkerchief. He blew his nose, rubbed it vigorously. From the sidecar he pulled out his long thigh-boots, bag and heavy double-barrelled magnum. He took the gun out of its canvas case and laid it down while he drew on his boots. He bent through the wires, stopping on the other side to open the gun. He wiped the oil from each chamber, dropped in the cartridges. After pulling back the hammers he closed the gun again. As he walked towards the far hedge his boots squelched in the wet ground, making him drag his feet slightly. Moisture hung on all the branches and twigs along the hedge. Single drops of water fell on the blue-black barrels, clung there.

Sounds came to him muffled in the heavy damp air as he went down to the bottom of the hedge, to stand beside a tall poplar. A train hooted in the distance, the sound not echoing but somehow getting caught for a second or two; a dog howled on the other side of the river.

He gripped the gun tighter when a snipe rose from the rushes at his feet. It zig-zagged over the floods, leaving behind its small scratchy cry. Jolly leant against the trunk of the poplar, looked up through the branches. Some last few leaves twisted and fluttered like dirty pieces of paper. His eye caught a movement, a pigeon. He watched until it had almost reached him. He put up the big gun, his left hand sliding along the barrel, waiting for the moment of connection when the bird is stopped, its feathers puffing and exploding, to drop, spinning like a shuttlecock to the ground. Jolly did not pull the trigger. The pigeon, seeing him at the last

second, swerved, down, and away on the other side of the
tree.

He lowered the gun and stared out across the water. The
wind made ripples on the flood waters. Further away he could
see a small pack of duck, black against the darkening colour
of the water. Rooks passed overhead cawing their slow way
to the woods behind. Jolly stepped out from the tree, went
into the water. His movements caused the ripples to widen
in front of him. The ducks splashed into the air. He found
a place to stand, behind a tall dead tree-trunk surrounded by
low bushes.

The dusk was now deepening, it would soon be dark.
There was no sudden change, just a slow almost mechanical
diminishing of the light. Things which had been clearly
visible were now vague, indistinct. A moorhen further up
the hedge occasionally squawked, the sound of a voice far off
came faintly over the valley. It was very still.

Jolly turned his head to listen more carefully. Was that
something? It would soon be too dark. There was no moon,
no break in the cloud. Darkness was coming in fast. There
it was again. 'Ayank, Ayank!' The geese were coming.

He opened the gun, felt for the brass ends of the cartridges.
He checked the hammers, quietly closed the breech.

There was no doubt about it, the geese were coming. He
pulled down his cap, shifted his feet, swaying slightly,
hunched, his head a little on one side, breathing faster.

'Ayank, Ayank!' They were very close now. They were
right over him, three dark objects. He heard the pellets rattle
against the pinions with the first shot. He fired again, waited.

'Ayank, Ayank!' They were past, their cries becoming
fainter again. Had he heard a splash? He came out and
looked over the water, listening. He did not move until he
heard a curious gurgling noise. It suddenly stopped. He
waded out as far as he could go. He saw the goose, floating,
its head now dropped below the surface of the water. He had
to wait until the wind brought the bird to him. He lifted
it out, shook off the water, and put it in his bag. It was now
quite dark as he started to walk back. Above him packs of

duck were flying upriver; he could hear the whistling of their wings. They called unceasingly, the short deeper note of the mallard interrupting the high-pitched keening of the widgeon.

When he got back to his motorbike he took off his boots, put the gun away and sat on the saddle. He switched on the torch, laid the goose out with its head placed on his knee. He let his hand rest on the neck for a moment. He stroked the still warm body, smiling quietly to himself.

As I Lay

Up they came every morning from under the window sill. Fishing boats moving slowly out across empty water. I watched from my bed. A broken column of black smoke went out with them, remained after they had passed from sight.

I was standing at the top of the beach. Early morning in April. I shivered in spite of the extra clothes. The stones on the beach were wet, from rain or spray. They looked cold. Down below, the sea stirred; a dirty brown swell. Grating shingle, audible from where I stood. There was cloud; possibly rain further out.

'Think you can be here by six-thirty,' the man had said. Well, here I was, hoping they hadn't left without me. Some boats had already gone.

The boy in the hut was bent over two flat boxes. He grinned as I entered.

'Can't think what's happened to the boss this morning. He's very late.'

'That's good,' I said, 'I thought I was.'

'No, you're all right.'

He bent again over the tray of frozen sprats. He picked one up, pressed the point of a large hook into the eye of the fish which slowly twisted as the iron went through the body. Small flakes of ice came off, dropped to the floor. The boy's finger's were red, raw. I sat down. Row upon neat row of baited hooks lay silver in the second box. They were attached, on short lengths of braided nylon, to a long line.

'Rather a cold old job,' I said.

'You get used to it.'

'I suppose you've been at it a long time.'

'Oh no, not so long. Couldn't stick inside work.'

'It must be pretty tough all the same.'

'Oh, you get used to it.'

The boss came into the hut, tugging on a bright orange oilskin.

'Morning,' he said, 'must have overslept. We'd better get a move on . . . do the rest on the way out.' He nodded in the direction of the bait boxes.

We went out to the boat which was resting on blocks beside the hut. I left the loading to them. They knew what to do. The open boat slid down the beach over greased sleepers. At the water, the boss told me to jump in, or I'd get wet. I clambered in over the high edge of the boat, sat on the centre seat by the engine. One of the other boats was waiting. A man threw a rope which the boy tied to a ring on the front. The boss and the boy stood behind the boat, pushed it down the last part of the slope into the water. They waded a few steps, jumped on the back end. There they hung for a moment, neither in nor out. They pulled themselves over the side. The boat had begun to swing round as the tow-rope tightened. The boy took hold of the starting handle, strained to swing it. The engine suddenly caught after a few turns. The boy went to the front, cast off the tow, waved to the other men. I remained on the seat in the middle. The wood vibrated through my whole body. The beat of the engine came through the rusty exhaust pipe like the quick firing of a gun.

The boss baited the remaining coils of line, stopping occasionally to put a hand inside the top of his oilskin trousers. The wind caught the thin curls above his forehead; his light-blue eyes wept with the cold. When he had finished, he took the tiller again, sat inertly, staring ahead. We seemed to be moving very slowly. Away from the shore there was little swell. The boat rose slightly with a wave, slid down again. Occasional splashes of spray came cold against the face. The noise of the engine made conversation difficult. My hands thrust deep into inside pockets, I tried to keep warm.

The boy unwrapped his breakfast, began to eat. He passed me a cup of coffee. It was not hot, but sweet and weak. He offered me a sandwich. I shook my head. I had eaten before coming out. He took off his oilskin jacket. Although we were well out to sea, we appeared only to have travelled a few hundred yards parallel to the land. Three other boats were still level with us, no longer very near. I could make out the shapes of the men standing up in the boats. I pushed my hands under my pullover, hard against the shirt. Slowly, very slowly, warmth returned to my hands.

The sky lightened, a misty cold-looking day. Spots of rain blew against my cheeks. The little wind was in our faces. We kept on straight out for nearly an hour, always within sight of the land. The boat did not move very fast.

We approached a red buoy. Right in front of it, the boat turned sharply to the left almost as if we had reached the junction of a road. Soon after, a smaller buoy showed above the swell.

The boss pointed.

'That's where we start,' he said.

'Are we in for a good day?' I asked.

'We might,' he answered, 'it hasn't been too bad the last week.'

I went to the other side of the boat, out of the way. The boy was rummaging around at the front, looking for something. He lifted out a short thick piece of wood with a metal hook at the end. He grabbed the buoy, which he heaved into the boat and quickly untied the end of the line.

'We've got about a mile of line down,' the boss said. He switched the engine into neutral. The boat hardly rocked. The boy started to draw in the line, his elbows going backwards and forwards fast. The boat gave a jerk as the boss put the engine into gear again. He took in the line at the back, coiling it into the boxes. He shook out the tangles, his movements smooth, unhurried. The line came in. At first, no fish. Just empty hooks. From some, small pieces of uneaten sprat still hung. The boss flicked them against the edge of the boat. Gulls gathered overhead, dipping and diving ceaselessly.

Their cries rose above the noise of the engine. The boy pulled in the line fast. Small fish he swung straight into the boat, crashing them against the front seat. The hooks came away, tearing the mouths. The fish fell to the floor. They moved their broken mouths, flapped against the wood. The boy took the gaff to the larger fish. The bottom of the boat filled slowly. The fish were mostly cod. Some large flatfish. Skate, the man told me. It was the other fish which caught my attention. The eyes. Pale green, opaque. Dogfish. With the large fin down the back, blunt heads, they looked like small sharks.

From time to time, the two changed places. The boss pulled in the line less jerkily, his greater height making the work easier. The front section of the boat slowly filled with fish; alive, slowly dying.

We came to the end. The new line was fastened to the marker buoy, tossed overboard. The boss stood at the back, twirling the line out of the flat boxes with a stick. The lead on the line took it straight under the water.

The gulls had remained with us, picking up sprats, occasionally a fish which dropped off as it was hauled in.

The boy took out a knife to clean the fish. I sat with the boss at the back.

'Nasty creatures, gulls,' he said.

'That's a job I don't much like,' he continued.

The boy had just opened one of the dogfish. Four or five baby ones moved weakly on the board. Their eyes too, were that strange milky green.

'Extraordinary, isn't it,' the boss said. 'Dogfish don't lay eggs. The little ones come like that. Nasty creatures, gulls,' he repeated, as the boy emptied the tray over the side.

'Do you know, sometimes in winter the little birds come and land on the boat, so tired they can hardly hang on. God knows how far they've travelled. The gulls wait for them. They must get thousands.'

'Have you always been a fisherman?'

'Yes,' he replied. 'Runs in the family. It's a mug's game these days. The big boys are the ones who make the money.

Trawlers. They clean up everything in the nets.'

'Would you fancy another job?'

'Don't know, really. I doubt it. Lucky to have the boy. Aren't many who're prepared to put in the hours these days. We're out nearly every day of the year. Bloody cold it is, sometimes, I can tell you.'

'I can well imagine,' I said.

'You'd better hop up the front again, if you don't want a wetting. Jump out, the moment we touch.' ...

'OK,' I said.

One of the other men was waiting with the rope. The boss and the boy pushed the boat out of the water. The drum at the top of the beach started to turn. We held the boat steady as it was hauled up the beach, pushed in the blocks at the top to hold it.

Several women already stood outside the hut, waiting.

The boy threw the fish into metal tubs, turned a hose on them. The tubs filled with water, light red in colour. He emptied the tubs, took the fish into the hut. He passed me standing beside the boat.

'Well,' he said, 'you going to sign on?'

'It's a tough old job,' I replied.

'You could be right there,' he said.

Sweet Chavender

Water slid from the sculls, was quickly swallowed by the current. The rowlocks squeaked as he lifted the sculls out of the water, as he bent forward again. He grunted at the end of each stroke, a grunt which was more of a dry bark than a grunt. Soon he settled into his accustomed rhythm, the boat moved forward jerkily. The bow dipped as he pulled, a ripple went out at both sides, smoothed away as the current caught it. He bent forward, pulled; bent forward, pulled; the boat moved slowly against the current. He worked his way steadily, a few yards out from the cement wall at the bottom of the river bank, towards the next slip. The rowing-boats, roped together in bunches, rocked slightly as he passed. It was end of season. The sign 'BOATS FOR HIRE' had slipped over sideways. From the river all he could see was 'BOATS FOR . . .' The sun came out for a moment, its light reflecting off the dull brick of a factory end-wall. He'd caught fish there.

He rowed on, keeping close to the bank where the current was not so strong. Occasionaly his scull caught the muddy end of a willow branch hanging down into the water. Once, the bloated body of a cat floated past, grey skin showing beneath the matted fur. He broke his rhythm for a moment to avoid hitting it. Slowly upriver. On the other side a woman was walking with her dog. Too far away for him to be able to see her face. For a while they moved more or less together. She sat down on a bench while the dog played round her.

He stopped rowing again. A barge passed, low in the water. He turned the boat sideways, held it steady as the wash came; it lifted the boat. The throb of the engines carried through the water, thudding through the boards below him. As the wash subsided, he brought the boat to face upstream, bent to the oars once more.

At this point the trees and bushes were thick on both sides of the river. On the right, behind them rose the roofs of houses. He could hear the traffic as he kept the boat on its slow upriver course. The traffic sounds faded again as he approached the next bend, disappeared when he turned it. He was nearly there.

He stopped rowing opposite the tannery. The wind – what wind there was – was blowing away from him. There was no smell. Two hundred yards further on children were splashing about in the shallow water of a bay, throwing sticks and stones for a dog.

He lifted out the sculls, laid them inside the boat. He dropped the anchor down, hand over hand, making no disturbance in the water. The boat slipped sideways until the rope tightened. There was enough current here to hold it steady. He stepped carefully over the seat, holding the side for balance, sat down again to face in the other direction. He remained thus for some minutes, breathing hard. He coughed, spat into the water. The blob of spittle floated away, rising and falling in the ripples caused by his movements in the boat. He put his rod together, pushing it away from him as he did so. He went through the same motions to thread the line through the rings. From a tin box on the floor-boards he took a made-up cast. As he picked up the thick red-and-white float, the single lead weight slid down the cast, bounced on the boards.

He looked carefully at the hook, ran the point across the nail of his thumb on which it left a tiny white groove. He coughed. Bending, he felt in his old canvas bag for the cheese. Hard, yellow cheese, old, strong-smelling.

He broke off a lump, kneaded it between his hands. The cheese crumbled into flaky pieces. Slowly it became softer as he rubbed it between his fingers and thumbs. He pressed the hook into the cheese, moulding it round the hook. It was a large lump. After wiping his hands on his trousers he lifted the rod. There was no need to adjust the float; he had been there before. The bait plopped into the water, sank immediately. The float was carried away by the current. It stopped, went under. He raised the rod, met resistance under water. He bent forward, pulled. Something moved at the end of the line, came slowly towards the surface. An old rusty tin showed above the water for a second; the hook came away as the tin rolled over, making a bulge in the water. The tin sank from sight again.

He reeled in, laid the rod down. There had been quite a disturbance in the water. On examining the hook, he found that the point had broken off. He tied on a new hook, dropped the cast on the boards, felt in the bag for his sandwiches. As he bit into the bread he could still smell the bait-cheese on his hand. He glanced towards the near bank. At the end of the swim, a backwater had formed round the trunk of a tree jammed into the clay bank. A raft of objects had collected, all pressed together: plastic bottles, twigs, a large white rubber ball, feathers, a boot, leaves. An occasional eddy swirled the whole mass.

A bell on the tannery roof rang out. He looked round. Figures emerged from the door facing the river. Some ran towards the bicycle sheds; the women moved briskly in the direction of the main gate. The bell stopped ringing. Voices came over the river to him although he could not understand the words.

Within a few minutes the yard was empty. Except for one man who was pushing the big gate shut. He walked back again, slamming the door as he entered the building. The sound carried over the river.

He put more cheese on the hook, picked up the rod. The bait dropped into the water. He let the line pass through his fingers, keeping a slight hold as it ran out. The float showed clearly above the brown oily water. He let the float go away from him for quite some way, held it steady. A tiny ripple went out at both sides of the float as the water divided round it. The float swung to the right and left as the current shifted.

He sat there, hunched forward; the rod in his right hand, the line lightly checked between finger and thumb of the left. The cigarette in his mouth burned down slowly. He spat it into the water. It hissed, went out. He coughed, reeled in. The bait had gone. He lit another cigarette, baited the hook, cast.

Half-way down the swim the float stopped. It jerked sideways, went under, for a second leaving a hole in the surface of the water. He waited, struck. Line went out fast, disappearing into the brown water. At the end of the first run he held harder. There was no need for care, it was not a big fish. He lifted the fish over the side, taking the line in his hand. He removed the hook, tossed the fish into the bottom of the boat. Its tail smacked flat against the floor-boards. The mouth opened and shut. He was not looking. He wiped his hand on a rag, put more cheese on the hook, cast.

Another fish pulled the float under almost immediately. A bigger one. This too he brought quickly to the side of the boat, pushed the net under it. He gripped the fish hard round the middle of its body. The big mouth opened. The fish made a dry sound, almost like a bark. He took out the hook, threw the fish down with the other one. Another cast. Soon there were fish all over the bottom of the boat, none of them entirely still.

The shadows lengthened across the river. He put another cigarette in his mouth, sat motionlessly in the boat. Water ran off the chain, down the inside of the boat as he raised the anchor, rested it a moment on the gunwale before heaving it into the boat. He sat down again, coughed.

The sculls dug in hard against the current, the boat moved downstream fast. The sun went off the water. A light mist rose off the surface of the river, he could see his breath. On down the river. The boat slid away from him at each stroke. Hard at the beginning, the sculls cutting into the water. He went quickly downstream.

He turned the boat across the river as he approached the landing-stage. The water slapped against the underside, he pulled harder till the boat faced upstream. He eased the boat in towards the float, brought it in against the pieces of black tyre nailed to the side. He stepped out, holding on to the mooring-rope. One of the cats came towards him, rubbed hard against his leg, went to the edge of the float. It miaowed, turned to look up at him.

He held the boat out, glanced round behind him. The other two cats came bounding down the bank. He drew the boat in slowly. The cats jumped in. Each caught up a fish in its jaws. The cats left the boat, ran up the bank again, with the fish-tails dragging along the ground.

He secured the boat, took out his things, leaving the other fish in the bottom of he boat. He walked to the top of the bank, stood looking down the river in the gathering darkness. Somewhere near him he could hear one of the cats eating a fish.

Day-Flies

The second day. I slowed down along the bumpy earth track. At the end there was just room to put the car in the shade of a tree. Dust blew past the open window. The wind rushed by: smoothing, flattening swathes of high grass in the meadows like wide lengths of rippling silk. The sun, already hot, was burning up the last of the morning haze.

I opened the back of the car. How the women in the shop had laughed as I attempted to explain what I wanted. Not that they had very much; not even butter. I had just pointed. They had packed what I required in rough grey paper bags. I laid the food in the grass where it would keep cool. The bottle of wine I pushed down into the river where the reeds were thick enough to prevent it from being carried away by the current. I returned to the car, took out what I would be needing. I drew on my high boots, adjusting the straps over my shoulders so that I could move easily. I picked up the other things, set off for where I intended to begin. I felt the sun warming the canvas of the waders. It would be good to enter the water. I moderated my pace, taking more leisurely strides. The long grass whipped against my legs: a dry sound. It was almost the only sound. Almost. Somewhere in the depths of the grass, the grating cry of a corncrake went along with me. Like the whirr-whirr of a sewing-machine. All the long week that sound never left me. It was not even a particularly pleasant sound yet it did not irritate. And always tantalisingly near. Not once did I see that tiny crouching bird which I knew only from pictures. One even-

65

ing a corncrake called just a few yards away from me at the point of an island in the river. I walked up and down, trying to find it. The bird stopped calling once or twice while another took up the cry on the far bank. I did not see it.

I walked on, more slowly, no longer tired after the long journey. The river was not visible from any distance. It meandered through the valley between high banks. On three sides of the valley, steep fir-covered slopes. The village lay on the fourth, behind me. I glanced back. The tall slender red steeple of the church stood out clearly on the hillside; beside it the dark walls of the graveyard.

I walked more slowly as I approached the river. The wind caught the willows and alders along the banks, blowing hard in my face, ruffling the surface of the water. I knew where I wanted to go. A startled pigeon flew almost into my face, went out low across the field, swerving right and left.

I kept away from the edge of the bank as I reached a long bend in the river. This was where I intended to begin.

The river ran deep here so that it was not possible to enter the water. I approached a thick bush, moved slowly to the edge. From this point I could see across the river. My dark glasses took away the glitter on the surface. I stood very still. The grayling would be lying deep in the water, resting like shadows against the bed of the river, moving slightly in the underwater currents. The clear water was dark-green in the deeper parts. Rings formed, widened on the top of the water as fish came up from the depths to take flies on the surface.

I watched. Mostly small fish. I was not going to cause unnecessary disturbance this time. It was still early. I could return later. I stepped backwards, not fast, until I was away from the river bank. I wandered on to a place further along. There was no cover at this point. I had to go down on my knees, working my way forward through the ripe grass. I took in the sharp fresh smell of crushed herbs. Meadow flowers brushed against my cheeks. Drops of perspiration ran down my face, steaming the glasses. I remained kneeling, took out a handkerchief, wiped the glasses clean.

I knew what I was looking for. I had to cast right across the river. Kneeling as I was, it was not easy to put out the line so far. I lifted the rod, moved the rod backwards and forwards. Each time I pushed the rod forward I released more line, carefully, unhurried. I was excited, but it was not the excitement of the day before. The line, with the tiny artificial fly on the end, came to rest on the water. It was almost too far for me to see. I reacted when I saw a movement on the surface. A small grayling. Not the one I had wanted.

I pulled in line. The fish suddenly jumped out of the water, tugged wildly. I looked again. A pike, also not large but larger than the grayling, was right behind. The pike followed fast but seemed undecided, as if it was puzzled at the grayling's behaviour. I took in line, wishing to spare the grayling. The pike appeared to make up its mind. It swung away, turned back to fasten on to the grayling at the side, taking the grayling halfway down the back. Both fish went down. I could no longer see them. Instead of one, I was now holding two fish. They came up again. The grayling broke free: momentarily. The pike closed in once more. I held hard, drawing both fish towards me.

Something gave. The line came back.

I could see both fish as they went down for the last time. They sank from sight. This was not what I had intended. I sat back on my heels, stretched out my legs, sat down properly. I watched for some minutes. I could see no signs of movement in the river before me. I rose to my feet, walked slowly back to where I had begun; a long ripple of rough water in the middle of the river where two currents crossed.

That was where I had lost a good fish the day before. I had been too hasty. Because of surface disturbance it was not possible, even with the glasses, to see down into the water. The fish was still there. I saw it break the surface, go back down again. The fish rose several times as I stood beside the bush, watching. I was going to do things better this time. If he comes, I'm going to wait, I said. I'm going to wait. I gauged the distance, deliberately taking time. I held the line in the air, coordinating my movements until rod, line and arm became part of one repeated smooth action. I let the line go out. It landed on the water. Wait, I said to myself. The fish came up, went down. He came up again immediately, right out of the water, shaking his whole length, splashing back. He used the high fin on his back as a lever against the current, trying to break my hold.

Again and again he came out of the water, the colours shining down his back. This time I made no mistakes. I eased the tired fish towards me, over the edge of the net. Slowly I raised the net. The fish lay still. I took out the tiny hook, not touching the fish. It lay in the net, barely moving, resting slightly on its side. I held the net against the bank, away from the current. The grayling righted itself. I pushed the net deeper into the water. The fish came out of the net, sank slowly, swam out into the deeper water, still half-carried by the current.

I wandered along the river again: there was no hurry. I approached a section of the river at which a long narrow island divided the river in two. Weed grew tall in the water but did not show above the surface. The bed of the river was pocketed with holes, some deep, some shallow. The long bunches of weed swayed together, swelling and contracting as the current caught them.

The day before, seeing a number of large fish there, I had unthinkingly rushed into the water. With the sun at my back, an enormous shadow had preceded me. Every time I moved, more shadows jumped. It had not been a very successful day.

I stood behind a tree for some minutes, taking in what I should need to think about when I was in the water. I stepped past the tree, sat slowly down. Taking care, I slid into the water.

Through the waders came the coldness of the water, refreshing. The current pushed against me, not hard, as I stood up to my thighs in the river. The main stream passed on the other side. I could see fish in the bare patches and breaks in the weed. They were rising to the surface unceasingly. I was out of the wind here. The sun burned my face as I stood in the river, watching, motionless. The head of a fish appeared for a second above the surface, disappeared. A huge head. Not even very far from me. I glanced round, changed my position so that I could throw the line behind me without catching in the trees.

The fly was on the water, moving over the spot where I had last seen the fish. I drew in line as the fly came towards me. I lifted the line off the water, held the fly in my hand, blew on the fly to keep it dry, waited. The surface broke, burst, throwing out waves some yards to the right of where I had seen the fish. Again that violence as the fish went down. I cast. Come on, fish, I said, come on.

As if responding, the fish went for the fly. I waited, raised the rod. A moment, a fraction of a second. Off, out into the river he went. Charging through the weedbeds. Going, going, going. He stopped, changed direction. I stood still, giving line when I had to; taking in when I could. I could not hurry the fish in the heavy weed. I had to think, try to anticipate. The minutes passed, the fish rushed less. I gained line. I saw him in the clear water, coming nearer each time he passed me.

I held the net under the water. He was in the net, struggling. A final quiver ran the length of the fish's body as I laid it out on the bank, still in the net. I pulled back the meshes to look. A big trout. Not young, already past its prime. The body not as fat as it should have been. It was time.

I swung the bag over my shoulders, walked along the bank, back to the car. I bent down, shook off my waders. I went down the bank. Walking was now so easy. I lifted the bottle out of the river. Cold drops of water ran off my hand. Sitting down in the grass, I picked up the knife, cut thick slices off the loaf. They felt soft and moist. I raised the bottle. The wine was so cold that at first I couldn't taste it. Just a cold, tingling sensation as I swallowed. I peeled the rind from the cheese, broke off a piece, ate it with the bread.

I sat on in the grass, with the sun shining down on me, eating, drinking wine. The wind blew against my face, still cooling.

Close Shave

Anyone for the sunny north, Dick said. Why not, I thought, haven't been back for donkeys' years, be a break from the Home Counties, go and look the old place up, it's only fifty miles from where I'll be. The old mind really started ticking over. Twenty years. My God, it's a hell of a long time; wonder what's happened to them all . . . John Peters, Roger Kirkpatrick, Tim Roberts, and what about what's-his-name . . . that Macalister fellow. The old mind really got going. God, I wonder what's happened to them all, bet they don't recognise me. I'll bet I've kept better than they have, stuck up there in the provinces.

It wasn't my fault, either, that things went wrong. Nothing but trouble, right from the start. I'm going to kick up a stink about that bloody car when I get back; three breakdowns in one day is a bit much, even for a company vehicle. Could have brought my own, I suppose, but that'd have put a lot of mileage on the clock, wouldn't have been worth it. Besides the company car's bigger, and that's an advantage all right. God, the traffic. I'd been away such a long time, I suppose I'd forgotten they had cars in the north; I can't have been more than ten when we moved. Back to nature, I must have thought. Stupid really. Actually, I didn't know the place I was going to at all, but in that part of the world all the towns are exactly alike: dirty, damp and absolutely dead. God, how dead they are. And the people on the streets, like a lot of black slugs.

Then, to crown everything, damn me if they weren't hold-

71

ing the annual fête or some other stupid local event the day
I arrived, so naturally there wasn't a room free at any of
the hotels. Christ, what a place, I thought, just my luck. If
there's one thing I can't stand, it's having to pig it when I'm
away on business. I'd had quite enough of digs in the early
days. Mind you, even now I've got my own flat, its nothing
to write home about, but at least it's your own mess and
nobody mucks you about. No landladies or any of that caper.

Anyway, there I was, stuck in the most bloody awful
traffic-jam, with nowhere to sleep and not much chance of
getting anything decent. And a car which kept packing up
on me. Not my idea of a joke at all, I can tell you. In the
end, I turned off into a side street and stopped outside one
of the shops. That was about the only bit of luck I did have.
The woman said she'd ask her sister who lived round the
corner.

Hoo-blooming-ray I said to myself when the woman nodded
at me while she was talking away, that's something. It was
cheap too, dirt cheap, and Mrs Oglesby was pleasant enough.
Too decent, really, ever to make a go of it. I was on expenses,
so I'd make both ways. The clients needn't know I wasn't
staying in the places we'd be eating at. In that respect, I did
quite well.

It was the usual sort of place, ghastly really, dark, like
entering the chamber of horrors. A long cavernous hall with
a monstrous hatstand, more like a dressing table, with a long
mirror in the middle. There were cracks running all over it
in crazy patterns. 'That'll do me nicely.' I said to Mrs Oglesby
when we went up to the bedroom. Two beds, another huge
cupboard, empty fireplace, black metal mantlepiece, green
wallpaper.

'Your tea'll be ready in ten minutes,' she said.

It wasn't, of course, but when it did come, there was far
too much of it, almost as if I'd been an unexpected guest.
Perhaps she felt she had to make a special effort since I was
a bit different from the usual type she got. Her husband
soon put me right on that one. 'Can't stop her,' he said, 'she
always makes too much.'

The only other person in the dining-room was a fat child. It was staring at the television set, quite motionless, its eyes huge behind thick-rimmed spectacles.

I addressed it; it made no effort to speak. It occasionally got up to take a piece of bread and butter off a plate on the table and then returned, chewing slowly until the round had been eaten. In fact, all the time I was there, I only heard it speak once, and then not to me. One of the other chaps there used to pull the boy's leg, but he just giggled, making his eyes even bigger behind the glasses.

Bill, one of the two lodgers, came in while I was sitting there. He had some sort of driving job which took him all over the place, I never did find out exactly what it was he was driving. Funny sort of chap really, terribly quiet, hardly opened his mouth at all.

He must have been about fifty, not very big, faded. You know what it's like with people who never do anything – or at least never seem to – like looking at a piece of butter, almost as if he was quietly disintegrating; though that's probably not how Mrs Oglesby would have described it if she had ever got round to thinking that far. He must have been a bit on the mean side, perhaps that's what it was. Always on the scrounge. He sat in every evening as far as I could make out, and every time Mrs Oglesby asked if anyone wanted a cup of tea, his weak voice would pipe up immediately, yes, he thought he could manage another cup. Still, at least he didn't stay down long. Nice company!

It was a filthy evening and I didn't feel like going out to see the sights. After the long drive I was quite happy sitting there watching TV in front of the fire (I ask you, a fire in August). I couldn't for the life of me remember what was on, but it helped the evening away. With the result that I got to bed far too late and was dog-tired the next day. My own bloody silly fault though. The other lodger, Rick something-or-other, poked his head round the door early on to say that he wouldn't be staying for a meal.

'Just as well you came,' Mrs Oglesby said, 'all that food going to waste. He's a right one.' she went on.

The old man came in shortly after nine, after shift. He had his meal, in silence, and afterwards lit his pipe beside the fire. He dropped off to sleep almost immediately. I sat on, too lazy to move, more asleep than awake, until the front door suddenly crashed shut. It was Rick. The old man sat up and started filling his pipe. Rick came in, nodded at both of us, and went over to the table to pour himself a cup of tea. What hair he had was all sticking up at the back. A smallish chap, very thin, with the most incredibly black eyes. A bit older than me, I thought. The old man, now properly awake, turned his attention to the screen and we all sat like dummies until the programme ended. Rick got up almost immediately and went out of the room. I followed soon after. And what a night it was, too. Black as pitch outside. My window looked out on to a backyard, an old tin-can kept getting caught by the wind, blowing up and down. Once a dustbin lid came off with a hell of a clatter.

The two sections of the old casement window rattled as if locked in a life and death struggle all night long. I must have dropped off to sleep eventually. What a place.

I had the dining-room to myself when I came down in the morning; for a while at any rate. Mrs Oglesby asked me if I'd have a cooked breakfast. I said I would. That was mistake number one. My heart sank when I saw what I was in for: two fried eggs, thick rashers of bacon, tomatoes, sausages, all in a nasty greasy mess.

'I hope you like a big breakfast.' Rick said, sitting down at the table. 'Just the usual, Mrs O. please. Don't you want to ask me who I was out with last night?'

'Shocking, it is, shocking. At your age, too.' I got the impression this was something of a regular performance. Rick grinned at me and went on trying to provoke Mrs Oglesby. When that didn't work, he turned his attention to me.

'I suppose you think this is a dead old town. Now, go on, admit it. Not quite what you've been used to?'

He went on, without waiting for me to answer. 'It's all a matter of what you make of it.' I certainly wasn't going to get involved in that kind of argument.

I didn't answer.

'What's in the news this morning? Usual bullshit, I suppose.'

Rick took his paper and went over to the sofa.

'Rick, you'll be late again,' Mrs Oglesby said.

'Don't you worry about me, Mrs. O.'

'Much use that'd be.' she said. 'You keep clear of him. He's a bad one.' Rick laughed.

'Don't you believe a word of it, she's biased.'

I sat on at the table reading my paper, and we didn't speak again until Rick went off. I was in no hurry, my first appointment wasn't until ten.

As it turned out though, it certainly wasn't the easiest of days and I began to regret having taken on this assignment. What a curious lot they are in this part of the world, with their built-in prejudices. All the executives I met seemed to be the same, all slightly on edge. I got the impression they thought I'd come with the express intention of stealing something from them, and not just to compare notes. One, in particular, I could have murdered. To start with, he kept me waiting, something which always gets on my nerves. Then, after shaking hands – why the hell they think they've got to break the bones in your hands when they do that is beyond me – he scuttled off behind his desk and sat there, as if waiting for something unpleasant to happen. And what a desk, too, a bloody great thing, solid as a tank, God knows how old. The top was as big as a normal dinner table, dark wood, with a raised section running the whole length; a clear line of division. This far and no further. Still, I managed to get the information I wanted in the end. What annoyed me most was that he knew his job like the back of his hand and had absolutely no need to be so bloody-minded.

The result was that I left the building cursing and swearing to myself. As I turned the corner on to the bridge, I nearly got blown over by the wind. Down below, a grey tide was flowing, the wind picked up flecks of foam, racing them along the surface. Grey-looking gulls skimmed over the swaying masts of small yachts moored out from the bank. I had to put my head down because the rain was getting in my eyes. I was still in such a temper over the interview that I walked for some time without thinking about the direction. Suddenly I hadn't the faintest idea where I was any more.

I stopped at a corner, tried to get my bearings. In front of me was a great wide empty street. Cars were parked side by side down the middle of the road. As I looked, the dark narrow window recesses took on the appearance of railway sleepers stretching away down the long perspective of the brick fronts. To the right was a narrower street with tall smoke-blackened buildings on both sides. Lines of washing hung across the street at various levels. I was so surprised at this sight that I stood there gaping. I wondered how it had been possible to hang things there, and how on earth the women took the washing in without soiling it. All the way down the street, the lines of washing jumped and twisted in the wind, like flags stretched across the road in honour of some event. Enormous washes: rows of pants, large and small, petticoats, overalls, shirts, nappies, pyjamas, blouses, jerking away for all they were worth between the straight-fronted houses which, in that narrow street, seemed to stretch up to the sky and blot it out.

There was hardly anybody about. An old man came towards me, hands in pockets, grey cloth cap pulled down over his forehead. He didn't even glance my way as he passed, his eyes bleary from the wind, a drop flattened on the end of his nose. He was round the corner before I thought of speaking to him. A child in a white summer frock rushed out of a dark doorway screaming 'Mam!' its face all screwed up. Out into the street and through another doorway. I heard its cries all the way up the stairs. They stopped suddenly. A pigeon was trying to walk along the middle of the road. It kept getting lifted off the ground by the wind.

I looked behind me and discovered that I was standing in front of a sweet shop. The chap inside told me how to get back to the town centre.

The rest of the day was one long rush, I didn't get back to my digs till pretty late. Rick and the old man were still up.

The old man was talking as I entered, Rick had almost disappeared in one of the easy chairs. One leg hung over the edge.

'And what have you been up to? Whoring?'

'Work.' I replied.

'More bloody fool you, then. Six o'clock's the limit as far as I'm concerned. No boss buggers me about.'

'I'm my own boss,' I said, 'for a few days anyway.'

'Well what're you doing out at this time of night, then?' he asked, sitting up in his chair and looking straight at me with those incredibly black eyes of his. They were astonishingly expressive, those eyes, and never still. I could see myself getting involved in an argument here, and I wasn't in the mood. I went over to the table and got myself some tea. I had interrupted one of the old man's monologues, and he soon started off again. It was a strange performance, the voice more often than not seeming to have an existence all of its own. Words, words and more words, the old days . . . hard times . . . I mean to say . . . a little bit of communism . . . the youngsters . . . slide-rule boys . . . I don't like the word, strike . . . industrial disputes. On and on and on, like listening to a faulty radio. Rick sat back in his chair again, slowly swinging his leg, not taking much notice – or not appearing to – only once interrupting the old man to say it all boiled down to three things: dishonesty, diplomacy and disillusion. The old man shook his head slightly.

'What kind of a bloody outlook is that?'

Rick didn't answer, he winked at me.

The old man coughed, grunted, banged his pipe on the palm of his hand, flicked the stem towards the fire, spat into the fire, then continued his monologue. I finished my tea and went out quietly.

Odd sort of bloke, that Rick, I thought, going up the stairs. God, normally, one thinks of going down to hell. Those green walls. The house wasn't dirty, either, it just looked dirty and it was all so bloody uncomfortable. No plug for the razor in the mornings, I practically had to swing on the light. One tap wouldn't work. There was hot water, very hot water, but only from the tap in the bath. And drops of moisture all over the walls, shining like spots of oil against that green. Damp, clammy sheets. God, what a place, and that bloody loo. It just had to be next to my bedroom. Rangle, tangle, tangle, every ten minutes, and a great swoosh of water. Doors banged, bedsprings exploded, boards creaked, squeaks, rumblings, boots clumping, like an army settling in for the night. Never again.

'Happy birthday to you . . . happy birthday, dear Rick, happy birthday to you.' Mrs Oglesby sang in a cracked sort of voice as she served breakfast the next morning. 'And how old are you today, Rick?'

'Twenty-five, Mrs O.' Rick replied.

'Yes, and the rest.'

'What do you mean?' Rick said. 'Just ask my mother.'

'I suppose you'll be out again tonight.'

'It's my birthday isn't it?'

He turned to me. 'You working tonight?'

'No.'

'If you like, I'll take you down to the club. You've got to be a member, but I'll get you in somehow.'

'You keep out of there, young man.' Why must women say such bloody stupid things.

'He'll be all right Mrs O., he'll have me to look after him.'

'What your wife would say about these goings-on, that's what I'd like to know.'

'How's my breakfast doing, Mrs O.?'

'You've always got an answer haven't you?'

'Just one egg, Mrs O. please. Now I'll pick you up here at about ten, OK?'

'Why so late?'

'Well, it's no good going down too early, is it?'

'I wouldn't know, I'm a stranger here.'

I got up to go, I had to leave earlier that morning as I was calling on firms outside the town. Actually, I did rather better than the day before; I suppose I must have been getting used to it, or something. But, God, how the weather gets you down in that part of the country. I've never known anything like it, not my idea of a holiday at all. I passed a bit of beach as I drove into one of the small towns along the coast, all the mums were out with the kids. Actually it was no more than a strip of shingle, the water all churned up a filthy black colour. Coal dust, I imagine. I remember in the old days we used to see people out on the beaches looking for lumps of coal. The kids were happy enough, kids always are.

I had a couple of hours to waste there in the afternoon, so I wandered down to the quay. It wasn't what you'd call inviting, a long grey pier stretching out on both sides of the small harbour, a line of people standing or sitting along it, fishing. I went towards them. They didn't catch much, mostly dabs. A lot of kids, too. One lad kept dashing backwards and forwards between two rods. He nearly threw himself into the sea each time he cast out the line with the heavy lead weight on the end. An older chap eventually came along to take one of the rods. The father. The whole family was there. The mother sat further along the pier with a smaller boy. Their holiday, I imagine. It was none too warm in that exposed place, I had to keep walking up and down. A couple of ten-year-olds were crouched on the slimy stone steps leading down to the sea. It looked dangerous, but they certainly weren't bothered. They'd got a tiny fibre-glass rod between the two of them, it couldn't have been more than three feet long, string as line, and some sort of home-made hook on the end. I actually saw them pull up a crab, which dropped off as it came to the surface. God knows what they'd have done if a big fish had taken the bait. The sea-swell moved up and down the steps all the time.

The men seemed to take it all very seriously, shouting at the kids if they started fooling around near their rods. Some of them were probably out of work, they looked it. You can never tell up there, most of the men go round looking like tramps. They weren't very talkative either when I asked if they'd caught anything. I wandered up and down the pier for a while, and as I left I saw the family gathered round

five miserable little dabs, none of them larger than one of
the kid's hands.

A right old game, I thought to myself.

I made my way back slowly, passing through a small park.
That was green enough. It ought to be, too, with all that
rain; hardly anybody about. A middle-aged woman was sitting
on one of the metal park benches, fiddling in her shopping-
bag. A bus-conductor in uniform was arguing noisily with
his wife, they lowered their voices as they came up to me.
Otherwise the park was empty, pretty bloody desolate it was,
some sort of statue in one corner, a grey, dirty-looking piece
of stone. And the flower-beds, all so neat and tidy, more like
a cemetery than a park. God, what a place.

As I drove along the coast road, the rain started once more.
By the time I got back, it was pouring. I dashed into the
house, catching a glimpse of myself in that crazy hall mirror,
hair all on end, forehead shining with raindrops.

'Nice weather you have here,' I said to Mrs Oglesby.

'Not very nice, is it.' she replied. 'Never mind, I'll have
your tea ready in a minute. I've got a nice bit of fish for you
today.'

It's anybody's guess what that fish had once been. It tasted
of nothing, smelt abominable. It was steamed into a white
flabby mess, with some equally flabby chips to go with it.
Still, she meant well. The digs were cheap, I'd certainly make
on the trip.

I decided to go and have a look round town after tea, I'd
got plenty of time before meeting Rick. The sky had cleared
a bit but there was still plenty of rain about. It was a miserable sort of street, leading off into other streets which all had
the same neglected air about them. Rows of small shops, the
usual things. It was none too warm, either. I went into a
pub, one of those drab corner houses. God, what a place, I
thought, but I was already in, or I'd have walked straight out
again. A completely bare room, three men at the bar, a dart-
board, a couple of plastic-topped tables, and that was it, just a
lot of space. Naturally, a TV set in the corner. I downed that
drink and got out quickly. I walked for some time, passing

several cinemas, but there was nothing on which I'd have wanted to see. Anyway I'd only have had time to see half the programme. I wandered along, more or less at random until I reached the more important streets. There wasn't what you'd call a main street, just several where the multiple stores and a few of the dreary larger local businesses were situated. I'd almost decided to give up and go home when I came to a bingo hall.

That'll kill an hour or so, I thought. Then I saw the notice "Members Only". The woman let me in without any fuss, didn't seem to give a damn as far as I could make out. It was a converted cinema, from which the screen had been removed. In its place was a huge illuminated board showing the numbers. In front of it sat the caller on his little throne. The place was packed, mostly women, a few elderly men. The most godawful smell of unwashed bodies, damp clothes and popcorn. Naturally I got it all wrong to start with, it was such a long time since I'd done it. The old woman next to me told me to wait until the green tickets were called. She almost snapped the words at me. I suppose it was a bit stupid. Eyes down. I ticked away, my mind only half on the job. The whole thing was so grotesque, that huge auditorium, the horrible lighting, rows and rows of bodies, heads bent until a line or house was called. Then the place came alive again, a sigh went all round the hall. The smell became insufferable, I got up after a while and walked out, having finished my last card. I don't know whether I'd have called if I'd had a winner.

'So that's where you spend your evenings.' Rick, of course.

'Just looking at the other half.' I said.

'Hey,' he said, grabbing my arm. 'Do you want to get your head kicked in?'

'Not particularly.' I replied.

'Well, you'd better watch it, then. I don't give a bugger, but some people wouldn't like it.'

'You could be right there. Things seem to be rather difficult up here.'

'Ah, it's not so bad. We may as well go down to the club now.'

Walking beside him, I suddenly realised that Rick was not as small as I'd thought, just very thin. He was terribly quick, too, you could never imagine him getting caught on the wrong foot.

We didn't have far to go. It wasn't much to look at from the outside. There was a brass plate outside, but it hadn't seen polish for a very long time. I just managed to read . . . men's Club, as we entered. Rick went ahead and got the tickets sorted out, five bob, he wouldn't let me pay. A great barn of a place, more like a drill-hall. Rick must have been looking at me.

'Not quite what you're used to, I guess. We're not so fussy up here.' he said.

A three-piece band was playing up the far end. A few middle-aged couples were moving rather lumpily round the floor, some of the girls were dancing together. There were tables, mostly unoccupied, beyond the crowded bar. Even when the music stopped, the noise was terrible. Rick was through to the bar in a flash. I followed. He bought the first round. He'd got himself a niche at the end of the bar, his back to the side wall, a place he hardly left all evening.

'My girl's here all right. Bloody annoyed with me too, I'll bet. I said I'd be here at eight. No good spoiling them. Keep them guessing, it's the only way. I rather fancy that one she's sitting with, though. I had my eye on her last week, wonder where she comes from. I'll find out. She's got a bloody good body on her. Pat's all right, but she's 28 and she's got four kids. She still likes it though. They all do, don't they?'

'Divorced?' I asked.

'No, you stupid bugger. It's her night off. You wouldn't know these things would you. The husbands don't mind, so long as there's not too much of it and things don't get serious. I bet that shocks you now. You married?'

'Not likely,' I said, 'I gather you are.'

'Has Mrs O. been opening her big mouth to you on the quiet?'

'No, you remember breakfast this morning. She mentioned it then.'

'Oh yeah. Well, I suppose I am a bit of a sod, really, but then I'm away all week. How come you're not married?'

'Never got round to it, don't fancy it somehow. I've never been caught so far.'

'I don't know about that.' Rick said. 'I've got a bloody good wife and three lovely kids. It may seem a funny thing to say, but I love my wife. She must realise what goes on, but she never asks. Christ knows what I'd do if I caught her at it. My mother still lives with us, so it's not so likely.'

'Evening Rick,' we were interrupted by a fat slob who'd been standing next to us for some minutes. A horrible creature, all guts and teeth, he must have weighed at least twenty stone.

'What'll you have,' he said, 'and your friend too.' He ordered. God, what a voice, a nauseating, grating sort of voice, it went right through you. He was on about life and how bloody it was. What a place, I was thinking. Rick was worse than useless, he stood there without saying a word.

'Well, we'll all be dead one day,' I said, wanting to try and change the subject. He put his beer down and looked at me with those horrible slob eyes of his.

'What kind of a fucking stupid remark is that?' he said. I shut up, just stood in front of him not doing anything. Then I turned to talk to Rick. Rick was rather absent-mindedly staring over my shoulder. Finally the slob moved off to join another group. Rick took me by the arm again.

'What's eating him?' I said.

'I don't think he likes the way you talk.' Rick said.

'And another thing. Don't you ever turn your back on a chap when there's trouble.'

'He was half-drunk, you can't argue with beer.'

'If I hadn't been standing beside you, you'd have been out cold. He knows bloody well that he'd have been smashed by my friends if he'd started anything here. But why didn't you tell him to fuck off?'

'What's the point,' I said, 'Christ, he was half-pissed. You

can't argue with a bloke in that state. It would have been
too bloody easy to tell him where he got off.'

'He wouldn't have said it to me and got away with it, I
can tell you.'

'It's not quite as simple as that.'

'You could be right there,' he said, 'Anyway, keep your
eye on him,' he jerked his head in the direction of the slob,
'You've got a friend for life there. What the hell, forget it.
Have another drink.'

'All right,' I said, 'but let me pay.'

'It's all on me tonight. What do you do, by the way?'

I told him.

'Good money?'

I told him.

'You clever buggers,' he said, 'it's always the same. I get
about twice what you're earning, sometimes more. Most of it
tax-free. Look!' He put his hand into his pocket and pulled
out a handful of notes, mostly fivers and tenners. Not so
much to show off as to prove his point. 'I've got a gang of men
here on contract. We go all over the country. I've been here
for about three months now. The firm don't bother me on
the job, they know me. Mind you, it's not all roses. You've
got to show the men who's boss, and there's only one way of
doing that in this line of business. They're a tough bunch.
It's a good old life, though. I do a good job and they can
take it or leave it.'

'It's rather the same with me,' I said, 'I travel round on
my own. I like the independence.'

'How old are you?'

I told him.

'Well, damn me, we're practically the same age.'

'What do you do with all that cash?'

'Well, the wife always gets her money. And I reckon I'm
a good enough father to the kids. They never go short of
anything. The rest, well, I'm out in the boozer most nights.
What the hell, it's a short life . . . oh, look out, here's more
trouble.'

Rick's girl. She didn't look too pleased.

'Remember me?' she said.

'Just having a drink with my friend,' Rick replied.

'I can see that. Going to make a night of it?'

Rick introduced me. She didn't seem very pleased about that, either.

'Who's your friend?' Rick asked.

'You'd like to know, wouldn't you.'

'Wouldn't mind.'

'You're a rotten sod.'

'We'll be over.'

'Aren't you going to buy us a drink?'

'I'm all right for the moment, thanks.'

'You bastard.'

'We'll be over.'

'You'd better be, you're not the only ones.'

'Women,' Rick said, looking hard in the direction of the other girl. 'I can see trouble there' he went on, 'I rather fancy that other one. Hey, don't you get thinking I'm the only bastard round here. They drop you just like that if they see someone else. You've got to take your chances . . . and make them.' he added.

'Well, how about it? Are we going over? I'll be breathing down your neck with that other one.'

I hesitated.

'All right, you don't have to say anything, it's written all over your face. Not your type, now, are they?'

I looked across the room. They were sitting opposite each other at the large table, just the two of them, each touching the glass in front of her, both a bit of a mess, not bad-looking, hair somehow all over the place; waiting for something to happen.

'They're not beauties,' he said, 'but they're all right.'

'It's not that,' I said, though it was true enough. I didn't really fancy the one or the other. I didn't know what I'd have said to them, either. They were married. Not my sort of thing, at least, not here.

'Yeah, well that's how it is isn't it?' Rick said.

'I'd better go over, i suppose, or they'll bugger off with

someone else, just to show me. I'll probably try and get off with that other one. I can see Pat's in a lousy temper. See you in the morning.'

'Yes, I'll be leaving tomorrow. Thanks anyway.'

I stayed for a few minutes to finish my drink before pushing through the crowd. I stopped in the doorway to button up my mac. What a bloody awful night it was. The wind had got up again. The lights over the middle of the road were blowing so that the shadows went up and down. Gusts of rain spattered against me as I set off.

'Just a minute, you bastard.'

Oh no . . . oh no . . . I said to myself, not that. He must have followed me out. He stood quite still in front of me, the shadows going up and down.

'What do you want?' I asked.

'I don't like you,' he said.

'Yes, all right,' I replied, 'now, let's forget it.'

He can't have been all that drunk. His whole body swung against me. He butted his head into my face, crashing my skull against the wall. His knee seemed to slip very slowly up my thigh. Oh God . . . I was on the ground, the lights were still going up and down, I heard voices, boys shouting. I could see his boot, a big black boot, it looked enormous. God, what a place, I thought.

Opposite Numbers

I was sitting by myself reading the paper. I like to go down to the centre of town, buy the paper and read it over a cup of coffee. The English papers are nearly always there in the afternoon. It really was hot, heavy, a storm not far away. The traffic on the other side of the cafe roared past. I looked up. The never-ending stream of people coming up to the pavement on the elevators started to blur into the grey sticky air. Even the pigeons mostly stood still; occasionally one would lift briefly off the ground and settle again. Two policemen bent over a drunk on the ground. He gazed up at them, clutching tightly two green plastic bags, his legs stuck out awkwardly in front of him. I could see the lips moving but I could hear nothing of the words. I found myself looking at a girl who was coming slowly towards me, a bag on a cord banging against her knee. She was carrying her shoes. I glanced down at her bare feet. I sat there watching the girl. She walked on quite unaware. She stopped, looked round the tables, most of which were occupied. She came towards me, stood still once more, at my table.

'Kann ich, bitte . . .' she stammered quietly.

'Ja, bitte.' I replied.

She sat opposite me, lifted the hand holding her shoes towards the table top, hesitated, then dropped the shoes on the ground. She placed the bag on her lap and sat staring out at the people passing by, her face quite empty of expression.

A waitress approached, stood beside the girl, her look passing down from the long centre-parted black hair, the floppy jumper, jeans, to the bare feet. The dirt showed between the toes. The girl sat very still.

'Was möchten Sie?' The girl turned.

'Eine . . . Kaffee, bitte.'

'Tasse oder Kännchen?'

'Wie bitte?'

'Tasse oder Kännchen?'

I pointed at my cup, and then to the pot of coffee.

'O, Tasse, bitte.'

'Danke,' softly, to me. Her eyelids dropped, closed, lifted again.

I picked up my paper and started to read, vaguely irritated. I suddenly discovered that I wasn't taking in what I was reading. I lowered the paper and found myself looking straight into the girl's expressionless eyes.

'Would you like to see the paper?'

'No thanks, it's just that I haven't seen an English paper for some time.'

'Are you English?'

'Yes.'

'You're very welcome to have a look,' I said.

'No thanks, I'm not very interested in the news. It was just seeing an English paper again.'

'Have you been here for very long?' The wheels started to turn.

'No.'

'Visit?'

'Not really.'

'What are you doing?'

'Au pair.'

'Do you like it?'

'It's all right.'

'What's the family like?'

'All right. Very nice, actually.'

'Do they work you hard? One hears stories.'

'No, not at all.'

'Can you get out when you want?'

'It's not so bad.'

'Is it a big family?'

'Three small kids.'

'What are they like?'

'Nice . . . very nice. I like children.' She seemed to mean it.

'What made you come over?'

'I got fed up, I suppose. Wanted a change.'

'Do you speak German?'

'Not much. You saw that. I'm supposed to be taking lessons. The woman I'm staying with has given me some books. But they all speak English.'

'I don't imagine you learn much from the children.'

'That doesn't matter. I like children.'

'Do the people take you out at all?'

'They don't go out much. They're very nice, they're much older, of course.'

'What do you do with yourself?'

'I don't know . . . I sleep a lot, come into town, like today, meet people.'

'Isn't it a bit difficult for a girl to meet people in a foreign country?'

'No, you meet people all right. I mean, I met you, for example.' The suspicion of a smile. It faded.

'Yes, but . . .' she looked up, opening her eyes wider than she had done till then. I didn't go on.

'How long will you stay over here?'

'I don't know, really, it depends. I'm in no hurry to get back.'

'What do your parents feel about your being over here?'

'My parents? . . . Oh, they don't mind. I've been working for some time.'

'What do you do?'

'I've had all sorts of jobs. I've tried quite a lot of things. I wanted to become a nurse, but I didn't have the qualifications. I even worked at a hospital for a while, but it wasn't the same. I left after a few months.'

'And then?'

'I had all sorts of jobs. I finished up in the country, on a

farm. Looking after horses.'
'That must have been pretty tough, not very well paid,
either, I should imagine.'
'It was all right, actually, I like horses.'
'Damned hard work.'
'I didn't mind. We were allowed to ride the horses, go
hunting.'
'You don't look the hunting type.'
'I like riding. I had a marvellous horse. The country was
beautiful.'
   'What made you leave?'
   'Oh . . . the usual thing.'
   'What was that?'
She sighed.
   'What made you take this au pair job?'
   'Seemed the easiest way to get abroad.'
   'Was it?'
   'Oh, yes. It was easy enough. I just replied to an advert
in one of the magazines. The only problem was references.'
   'Didn't you have any?'
   'No.'
   'How did you solve that one?'
   'A friend wrote some for me.'
   'Wasn't that a bit risky?'
   'Not really, I told the woman after I got here. She didn't
seem to mind.'
   The waitress came with the coffee. She put it down on the
table, so hard that at least a third slopped over into the saucer.
It didn't seem to bother the girl, if she even noticed. She
picked up the cup and as she tilted it to drink, drops of
coffee gathered on the bottom rim, dripped on to her jeans. I
took the saucer and emptied it on the ground.
   'Thanks,' she said.
   'That waitress was damned rude.'
   'It's all right. I didn't really want the coffee, but you have
to order something, I suppose.'
   'So you don't know how long you'll stay?'
   'No, not really, I'd like to see some other places while

I'm here. I've seen some pictures of Munich. I'd like to go there sometime.'

'Au pair again?'

'Might. I wouldn't mind trying something else. Hotel work perhaps. A friend of mine did. He said he'd help me if I wanted something like that.'

She pushed up the sleeve of her jumper, rubbed her arm, and then abruptly pulled the sleeve down again. She put a box of matches on the table.

'Cigarette?' I asked.

'Thanks,' she said. She had an odd way of holding the cigarette, as if she wasn't used to smoking. She pulled in her lips with each short puff. She stubbed out the cigarette when it was only half finished.

'Another cup of coffee?'

'No thanks.'

'God, this heat's terrible.'

'I suppose it is rather hot. I like the heat. I think perhaps I'd better be getting back.'

I called the waitress and paid.

'You'll be here then for some time?'

'Oh, yes.'

'Are you on the phone?'

'Yes.' She wrote the address down for me.

'Well, it's been nice meeting you. Cheers,' I said.

'Cheers.'

Dog-Days

Now I reckon to be a pretty easy-going sort of bloke, but when one of your own mates drops you right in it, it really chokes you off. A dirty rotten trick it was. It fair beats me why he should have done it at all. There we were, me and the lads, Saturday night, all ready to go. Ron – that's the one – said he'd be along later if we hadn't got fixed up. He had to go and fetch his girl . . . said she lived somewhere out of town. I have to admit that old Ron has got his uses. It's an absolute marvel the way he can chat up a girl . . . any girl. I don't bother about that sort of thing quite so much these days, but once in a while you get a bit itchy. Well, it's human nature isn't it, as Ron would say. He would. He's always got an answer. Last weekend, with Mavis and the kids off at her mother's, I just felt like a break. A little bit of fun on the quiet. No harm, either way. Now that Ron, he's a rotten sort of bastard when you come down to it. I mean, he's out practically every night, knocking off someone else's missus. Tells his wife he's on duty. Some duty! Still, as I say, he's got his uses, and he is good company. No getting round that. I reckon he could have any woman he wanted. But it's a funny thing; he doesn't seem to be all that choosy. Never seems to get hold of anything special. At least, not the ones I've seen.

There we all were, at the Anchor. That's our regular. Good place it is too, to pick up a girl. Lots of holiday-makers. Not that there's ever any shortage in the season. Mind you, nowadays I generally only go down for a drink. We got off to a good start though. Couple of girls up at the bar when we came in. I noticed the one straight away. In a long dress with no back to it. The front wasn't bad either. Not bad at all.

'Up for the week?' I said.

'Yes,' the other girl replied, and we were away. The younger one was already talking to two lads. They looked like school-kids. And they didn't like us moving in at all. Well, we soon got talking to the one; Rose, she said her name was. Her friend wouldn't tell us, but Rose whispered that she was called Pat. Pat was interested all right, but she hadn't made up her mind what she wanted. That was pretty obvious. We had a few drinks and seemed to be getting things fixed up nicely. Pat still wasn't exactly encouraging, but she didn't give us the brush-off either. Rose chattered away, but I think she somehow sensed we were more interested in her friend. Quite small she was, a slightly frightened look about her. She drank rather fast and began to laugh a lot. Nervous perhaps, or just not used to drink. Her friend kept looking round the room, not at anyone in particular, as if she was expecting someone.

I rather got the impression Rose had taken a fancy to me. I played along with it. Why not, there was plenty of time. I thought I'd get Pat round eventually, even if we had to take both girls along with us.

Old Ron finally put in an appearance. Alone. He seemed a bit annoyed. He'd missed his girl somehow. He always hates getting ditched, though he said it was just a misunderstanding.

Rose was putting it on a bit thick by now. Laughing at everything we said, although we weren't being all that funny. Mind you, under it all, I think she was getting a little impatient. So far we'd made no move to leave the bar and it must have been pretty obvious where our real interest was.

And that's when Ron had to go and put his great hoof in it. 'Well, how about us taking these two girls to a Disco'?' he said. Actually, there was nothing wrong with that, but he was giving me a bit of a look, which I didn't quite take

in at the time. Trouble was, Pat didn't want to go with us . . .
and finally said so. Even old Ron couldn't get her round.
He'd come in too late. And then Rose started to back down.
She came closer to me and said:

'Look, I think I'd better be getting back . . . you don't
really want to go out just with me.'

'Don't be daft,' I said. I mean, well, what could you say?

'It's OK, love. Just you wait here. I'll be right back, and
then we're off.' I meant it too. I left the bar with Ron.

'And where might you be going?' he asked as we came out
of the Gents, and I turned in another direction.

'Off!' I said.

'Hey, you can't do that,' he went on. 'That Rose has got
her eye on you. She wants a bit of fun.'

'Yeah, but it's the other one I fancy.'

'You stupid bugger! There's bitch written all over her.
You'll not get anything out of that. Didn't you see her sizing
up anything that came into the bar. You're wasting your
time!'

He grabbed me by the arm. The swine. I can't think why
I let him do it. Who does he think he is? Kind of local Sir
bloody Lancelot.

'Now love,' he announced. 'You're coming along with us.
And you'll have a lovely time . . .'

'With you!' he muttered to me.

Talk about gratitude. Her sad little face fair lit up, it did.
So that left me right in it.

We left the bar, just the three of us. The other lads stayed.
I knew they were laughing. It was all over their ugly faces.
Joke of the month.

It wasn't much of a night as we walked, arm in arm, along
the street. Not exactly cold, but the breeze coming off the
sea felt damp. There were plenty of people about, come in
for Saturday night. Or just holiday-makers. Old Ron kept
nattering away. I could feel Rose holding on to my arm.
She really gripped hard. She looked at me, too, from time
to time. I could sense it. I didn't say much. Let Ron get on
with it, I thought.

The Disco' was packed; it always is at the weekend. Not really my sort of thing these days, but you've got to play along with what they want. Can't have it all your own way. Ron soon found an excuse to slide off.

'But you're in very good hands with my friend here!' was his parting shot. And that was that. While the music played there was such a noise that talking was almost out of the question. Not that she seemed to want to. I offered to get some more drinks. She said, all right, but was I going to come back. And that look. She wanted to come with me, but I said she'd better stay, or we'd lose our seats. It took me ages to get served in that crowd. When I returned she was still sitting in exactly the same position, as if she hadn't moved all the time I was away. We had a drink. Not a word: she just sat there, holding my hand.

'How about a dance, love?' I asked.

'Oh, I'd like that.' she replied.

She even danced in a very odd way. All by herself, almost as if I wasn't there. She didn't move very much, just seemed to – how shall I put it – sway on the spot, elbows in at her sides, arms held out in front of her, fingers limp. She kept her eyes tightly closed and let her head go slightly from side to side with the music. She looked as if she was in a trance: the one quiet spot in all that wild crowd.

'Shall we sit down?' she said, opening her eyes, as if she'd just woken up.

'Tell me about yourself,' she said.

'You're married, aren't you?'

'Yes,' I replied.

'I like that,' she said, 'You answered me. . . . You've got a nice smile. Kind! . . . But I don't much like that friend of yours.'

'I'm beginning to feel the same myself' I answered.

'But, what about you, what sort of a week have you been having?' I said.

'Horrible . . . horrible.' she answered.

'Stuck here all day, every day, with the kids. It's worse than being at home. They never give me a moment's peace.

Rowing from morning to night.'

'What about your husband? Isn't he here?'

'No! And he said he was going to come at the weekend, too! It's always the same. He's always working . . . or says he is.' she added in an undertone.

'Well, you've got your friend with you.'

'Yes, but she's here on her own. Said she'd help me with the kids. She's a neighbour of ours. But it was only an excuse to get away from home. She's out by herself every night. She only suggested we go out together tonight because she had a fit of conscience. She's so attractive.'

'What about the other people in the hotel?'

'Oh, you know what it is. Mostly old couples, apart from one chap on our floor. He must be about seventy and he keeps on pestering me. He even knocked on my door last night. I keep it locked now.'

She stopped speaking, turned her head slightly to look at the crowd. The dance floor was again so full that it was almost impossible to move. A slow number. With the lights dimmed, it was difficult to make out anything more than a slight sense of movement in all that mass of bodies. Rose pressed my hand, leaned towards me.

'I am enjoying this,' she said.

'That's nice,' I replied.

'You've been very nice to me,' she went on. 'Look,' she continued, 'come back to my room. We'll have a drink together. Let me treat you for a change.'

Christ, I thought, now what.

'All right,' she went on 'You don't need to say it. I know what you're thinking. But you will take me back to the hotel, won't you? I'm feeling a bit tired. It's been a hard week.'

'Of course I will.'

The streets were much emptier now. A cold drizzle blew in from the sea. Rose held my arm, pressing her head against my shoulder. She stopped suddenly, her face white against the pale street lighting.

'You will come up for a drink, won't you? . . . Please.'

'Look, love,' I started to say.

'Go on, be a dear.'

'Look, I . . .'

'Oh God, you're all the same. What was it all about then. Lay it on thick till it comes to the point. Then you don't . . . or won't. Don't be so bloody staid.'

Staid, she said. What a word.

'OK, love. Let's leave it at that.'

She pulled her arm away from mine. We walked back to the hotel in silence. At the entrance, she looked briefly up at me, went to go through the door. I pulled her back, kissed her on the cheek. It was cold, damp from the night air. She went off without a word, not so much as a glance. I could really murder that Ron. Of all the dirty, rotten tricks.

Still Life

He could see cars all the way up the drive. There was nobody in sight. He stopped behind the gate, remained standing, his head slightly turned. Sounds just reached him from the other side of the house. He walked on, up the long drive, the gravel crunching against the soles of his shoes. With his thoughts elsewhere he looked round, only half-seeing the sunlit garden bright with summer flowers. Neat beds skirted lawns stretching away to the darker greens of trees, hedges. He went on, past the old white lilac on which were still some few last fading blooms.

At the door he pulled the bell, waited unthinkingly for the tiny interval between his pulling and the hollow ring at the back of the house. The house seemed deserted. He took hold of the metal bell-pull again, rang. He heard footsteps approaching. The door opened.

'Oh, Mr John! There you are! We'd quite given you up.'

'Hello, Mary. I am sorry to be so late. I just wasn't able to get here in time.'

'You poor dear, but why on earth didn't you come right on round? You know the way.'

'I . . . I thought I'd better ring. I am awfully late.'

'Well, you're lucky anybody came at all. We're all in the garden. I'd just gone into the kitchen for some glasses and I heard the bell. We've got a marquee on the lawn. It's all very grand. Oh, Mr John, it was such a beautiful ceremony.'

'I'm so glad. I got held up.'

'What a shame. Miss Julia looked lovely, quite out of this world.'

99

'I'm sure she did. And how are you keeping?'

'Well, none of us is getting any younger, but mustn't grumble. Mrs Smythe has been poorly of late, very poorly.'

'I am sorry to hear that. . . . Shall we go on through?'

'Of course, Mr John. But let me take your hat. You'll not be needing that.'

Mary turned, her starched white apron crackling with the sudden movement. After the sunshine, the house, with its low ceilings, was dark, almost cold.

'There you are, Mr John,' Mary said, as they reached the lounge, 'I'll be leaving you. I don't have to introduce you to anyone here. I've still got to get those glasses.'

'Thank you, Mary, I can make my own way now.'

The wide french doors were open. John looked out. Most of the several hundred guests were assembled in groups near the marquee at the end of the lawn. The black of the men's morning dress stood out against the lighter colours of the women's clothes. There was movement, animation. John stayed where he was, motionless. Conversation, laughter, came to him, not muffled but not clear. The guests were too far away for him to recognise anyone.

He shook his head as if waking, walked down the steps into the garden. The sun beat down, making him blink, working through the thick material of his suit. He moved forward on the lawn. Under his feet the grass felt soft, giving slightly as he walked.

As he approached the main group of guests he was touched lightly on the back. Somebody's hand rested on his shoulder.

'Hello, stranger. Just come?'

'Yes,' John replied, 'I didn't quite make it to the church.'

'Bad luck, old man. Nice to have you here. Oh, excuse me . . . we must talk later.'

'Fine, Bill, I'll look forward to that.'

John continued to pass through the crowd. He caught scraps of conversation, began to recognise faces. There were tables in front of the marquee with food on them. John took a glass of champagne from a tray. To get out of the sun he

walked to the end of the marquee where he could stand in
the shade of a tree.

Somebody knocked on a table three times, repeated this.
The guests began to draw nearer to the marquee. Three
times, more slowly, the table was knocked again. The sounds
of conversation slowly died away. The bride and bridegroom
approached each other in front of the tables, turned to face
the guests.

A man John did not recognise began to speak. John
listened. All words he had heard before. They seemed to come
almost singly, unconnectedly:

'. . . this joyful occasion . . . lovely bride . . . lucky man
. . . our friends . . . not losing . . . but gaining . . . long life
. . . together. . . .'

John's gaze passed over the faces, the motionless silent
crowd. Occasionally laughter broke, the slight breeze lifted
the hem of a dress, a hand went up to a hat. He looked
towards the bride. Her face was caught in the brilliant sun-
light, the whiteness of her dress reflecting upwards. In her
clasped hands she held a small bouquet of yellow roses.

Her eyes were directed unswervingly at the speaker,
although her features remained quite still. Even when he
turned to address her, the expression on her face did not
change. Once, the bridegroom put his hand out to her, let it
fall when he saw her still contemplation.

The man's speech ended. He said something amusing
which provoked a roar of amusement from the crowd. Glasses
were raised as the toast was called. The bride's hands
tightened momentarily around the bouquet; she raised her
head slightly. Expression returned to her features, as if she
was emerging from a dream. Turning, she smiled fleetingly
into the crowd, acknowledging their good wishes. For a brief
moment she looked directly at John although, because of the
sun, she could not see him.

There were more, shorter speeches. At the end, guests came
forward to offer their congratulations. John waited his turn.
The crowd gathered at the tables, serving themselves. John

found himself enclosed on all sides. It was not easy for him to make his way through the press.

The crowd was so thick round the bride and bridegroom that they became separated. John came close to the bride.

'Hello, John. You came. I looked for you in church.'

'I wasn't there. I'm sorry, it wasn't possible.'

'Never mind, you're here now. Will you stay for the dance?'

'No, I have to be getting back. It was difficult to be here at all.'

'I'm sorry. Thank you ïor your present. I shall treasure it. You're very generous.'

'I'm so pleased you like it.'

Julia held out her hand. John took her hand, held it briefly. He lifted his eyes to hers. She was looking steadily at him.

'Goodbye, Julia.' he said.

'Goodbye, John.' she replied.

Past Tense

It's a funny thing, but people always seem to come and talk to me. I don't ask for it, don't provoke it, yet somehow it happens. Often when I least expect it. Take Richard, for example. We've known each other since college, married about the same time, both have two children, roughly the same kind of job. Our offices are even right next door to each other. We're very good friends. Perhaps that's the reason why we've never talked about our private lives. That is, till last Wednesday.

There wasn't very much going on. I was thinking vaguely about what ought to be done but not actually doing anything when there was a knock on the door. Richard came in.

'Hello Nick. Busy?'

'Up to my eyes, old man.'

'Yes, I can see that.'

'Never too busy to spare you a few moments. Come on in.'

'That's decent of you. I don't think.'

'Hmm . . . what's on your mind?'

'Got a bit of a problem . . . and I don't quite see what to do about it.'

He sat down by the window, turned to look out over the roofs. He opened his mouth to speak, hesitated.

'It's very odd . . .' he began.

'What is?' I asked, quietly.

'It's the last thing I'd ever have expected . . . I don't really know where to start.'

'Why don't you start at the beginning.'

'If only I knew where that was.' He sighed, rubbed his eyes, brought his hand down over his nose and mouth.

'I don't think I need say too much about my married life. What you don't know, I'm sure you've guessed. I don't suppose it's any worse than most, and probably better than some. In the beginning it was even quite satisfactory; quite good, actually. It's been a sort of slow but steady drifting apart. Yet there was always a little something there: even if no real contact any more. I don't mean physically. That was all right, although that too has become less with the years. But we'd got the kids, the family, masses of common friends, hobbies. I won't go into all the details. It wasn't even a rut. At least I don't think it was. Or was it? It's awfully difficult to say.'

He paused, sat motionless, stared unseeingly out of the window.

'Of course there were the odd lapses; I won't deny that. But nothing very much. Certainly nothing that mattered. To me, that is. And I don't think there were any hard feelings one way or another. . . . To be quite frank, I'd got fairly used to the way things were. You see, perhaps it was a rut. Who am I to decide?

Anyway, we'd been invited out – to a wine and cheese party. Some months ago. Absolutely everything went wrong that day. The car broke down, one of the kids cut herself – rather badly, actually – I wasn't there, oh, and I don't know what else. We had one hell of a row. And that's unusual. Then Mary said she was damned if she was going to any party. With me, that was. I suppose I should have been more understanding, but I got all steamed up, and decided I wanted out. As a matter of fact I didn't even know the people who were giving the party all that well. Met them at the tennis club. They only moved here recently. They seemed rather pleasant.

It was the usual sort of do. Lots of people milling around making a terrific noise. I wasn't in a very sociable mood, wandered round in something of a daze. I spoke to a few people from the club. Got into conversation with some neigh-

bours of ours. . . . I can see it now. I was standing near the
door, only half-listening to what was being said. A couple
entered. I looked at them casually. An oldish chap – actually
he can't be all that much older than me – and his wife. At
the time I didn't know it was his wife. She looked so
incredibly young. I was suddenly furious. With the pair of
them. Quite ridiculous. I had never seen them before.
   They went on in. . . . I began to take a little more interest
in what was going on, forgot all about them. . . . Normally I
wouldn't have stayed very long, but the mood I was in I
didn't want to go home either. I moved round a bit, eventually found myself a seat on the floor, at the side of a large
open fireplace. I sat with a glass in my hands staring into the
fire. It was a huge room. The lights had been turned down,
so that the fire threw quite a glow. People were jabbering
away, arguing about something or other. You know what it's
like. Some people just have to prove how brilliant they are.
I made a few unserious comments, which didn't go down at
all well, then relapsed into silence. Left them to it. Almost
dropped off to sleep.
   'Enjoying yourself?' somebody whispered in my ear.
   'Er, yes, of course.' I mumbled. It was the girl who had
come in earlier.
   'Do you like parties?'
   'Normally, yes,' I replied, 'but I'm not wild about this one.'
   'I hate them,' she whispered.
   She turned to her husband, appeared to be listening to the
fatuous conversation going on among the group by the fire
although she made no contribution to the discussion. I tried
not to listen, went back to looking into the fire.
   'Is your wife here?' The girl was up against my ear again.
   I had to laugh. 'How do you know I've got one?'
   'Oh, most people do. Is she here?'
   'No.'
   'Why not?'
   'We had a row.'
   'I'm sorry.'
   'That's all right.'

Her husband got up, so that there was a little space between us and the rest of the group. It was a most curious situation. We sat there, the two of us, talking. Not even looking at each other. Anybody glancing in our direction would have assumed we were sitting, speechless, almost hypnotised by the fire. I can't remember much of what we said, either. Our words got swallowed up in the noise of the party all round. She told me something of herself, not much. She'd married young, but wasn't as young as she looked. It was very peaceful sitting there. I realise it's a strange thing to say, but it's true. Except, that is, for the odd questions she from time to time asked. We'd been talking about something quite different when she suddenly said, 'Do you love your wife?'

I made no attempt to answer her question. I am not sure that I could have, anyway. My mind went completely blank.

'I'm sorry, I shouldn't have asked. I'm very direct.'

'I was just rather surprised.'

'Can you remember numbers?'

'Why? You do ask the most extraordinary questions.'

Her husband bent over to say that it was time for them to go. She glanced briefly at me, whispered a telephone number. I didn't see her again. I suppose they must have disappeared pretty quickly. I didn't stay on very long after that.'

He stopped, appeared to be at an end.

'Is that all?' I asked.

'Not quite.'

'What happened?'

'Good question. Nothing really.'

'Did you phone?'

'Yes. Though I wasn't sure whether I should have. You never know with casual meetings like that. And it was such a strange evening.'

'But you did meet?'

'Oh yes, though it wasn't easy. If you haven't got some sort of travelling job, it's difficult to find time. Time gets shorter and shorter. Anyway, we arranged to have a meal. The place was no problem. Although it's funny how self-conscious you

become when you don't want to be seen. It was a bitterly
cold evening and there weren't many people about. With
the Christmas decorations along the street and the lights I
felt extremely conspicuous. Rather silly, really. Then she
was a bit late and I had to keep walking round the square.
I began to get some pretty dirty looks from a woman waiting
for a bus. I wasn't even too sure if I'd recognise her. But she
did finally come.'

He paused. I waited. He looked up at me.

'I suppose you want to know the rest.'

'If you want to tell me.'

'Well, there isn't very much. Again, it was so strange. I
hardly knew the girl. We hadn't really spoken at the party.
It could have been dreadfully embarrassing. But it wasn't.
We talked easily, as if we'd known each other for years. There
was absolutely no tension. . . . She couldn't stay very long.
One of the neighbours was baby-sitting. I walked her back
to the car. It was absolutely bitter, the wind cut right
through. We got into the car together. I have to laugh when
I think about it. I'm getting a bit old for sitting around in
cars. It was so cold we clung together, more for warmth than
anything else. Although that wouldn't be quite true. It was
more like two children cuddling.'

'Have you seen her again?' I asked.

'Once or twice. It's such a problem arranging to meet.'

'Are you in love with the girl?'

'Love. . . . I don't know. I haven't really thought that far.'

'What do you want me to say?'

'I'd rather you didn't say anything.'

'Well, you could be pretty sure I wouldn't, couldn't you.'

'Yes, that's why I came to see you.'

'All Change!'

'You know, it's funny, I was just saying to George the other
day. . . . Another beer? . . . Think I will. . . . Hadn't been
out of the office for ages. You know how I hate travelling. And
of all places, that northern branch. It just had to be me, too,
with practically everybody on holiday. Oh well, I thought, it's
not the end of the world . . . though in a manner of speaking,
I suppose it is. God, how I hate leaving London. And that
ghastly train journey. To make it worse, I had to be back
the next day, and that meant travelling all night. Wasn't even
a sleeper, and three changes into the bargain. What a life,
eh? Oh well, you can't win every time. Had to take someone
with me, too. Our Jean. Yes, pretty little thing, isn't she?
So at least there was a bit of company. Though I have to
admit that I slept right through to Crewe on the way up.
But then we set off at some ungodly hour of the morning.
You know how I detest getting up early. Had quite enough
of that in the war.

Well, we got there eventually. Round about midday, I
suppose. Just to be on the safe side, I'd taken a suitcase with
me. Never know on these trips; the railways being what they
are. I popped it in the Left Luggage; didn't want to cart the
damned thing round with me all day. According to the
notice, open till ten in the evening. That'll be all right, I
thought. Can't stand being cluttered up with bags and bag-
gage. And you know what a touchy lot they are up there.
Might have thought I was off on holiday, or something. Some
holiday! Jean had organised a lunch-time meeting. Suited
me.

What a gorgeous day it was. Extraordinary, really. Somehow one never expects the sun to shine up there. And when
it does, it's such a half-hearted affair. But it really was hot.
Too damned hot for me in my suit, I can tell you. I seemed
to remember the restaurant was somewhere near the station,
so I suggested we walk. Expressly told them not to meet us
off the train. Felt a walk might be pleasant after the journey.
Course I got lost. Even up there, they seem to be tearing
everything down. I missed my old landmark. That big
granary. You know the one. Way of all flesh, I suppose . . .
or rather, old brick . . . if you see what I mean. Streets all
looked the same. God it was hot. Well, we eventually got
there. Italian place. Naturally. Can't trust English cooking
that far north. Even so, it was still a bit of a blunder. Most
odd sort of place. Split in two. One half for the plebs – Pizza,
that sort of thing. Pretty packed, too. And then the
restaurant proper on the other side. Our side was absolutely
empty. Dark, murky place, with a very low ceiling. And heavy
red curtains round the walls. Reminded me of those French
films we used to see in the old days. Chaps taking their
mistresses off to obscure restaurants with special rooms at the
back. You remember, I'm sure. There we were, just the
three of us. The local manager joined us almost immediately.
Of course the waiters couldn't do enough for us. The service
was excellent . . . old-fashioned, in the right way. So much
so, it seems a little unkind to complain about the food. What
was it they called the thing I had . . . 'Dish of the House',
or something equally ridiculous. Course I didn't say anything. You know how sensitive they are. That fish must have
died a long time ago. They'd covered it with something that
smelled like petrol. God knows how I got it down. And the
wine . . . Ugh!

Heavens, why am I telling you all this? I'm being a fearful
bore. Oh, I know. It was what happened later. Actually, we
got through the business part quite well. Absolutely no
problems. I must say Jean was marvellous, an enormous help.
So I asked her what she'd like to do in the evening. I offered
to take her out for dinner. She said she'd prefer to have a

quiet beer somewhere. You know what these girls are about their figures.

Altogether there was something really odd about that whole day. I find it awfully difficult to put it into words. The local manager told us of a good pub near the station. Suited us fine. Great big place it was. Underground. We had to go down a sort of spiral staircase. At the bottom we entered an enormous, cavernous beer-hall which appeared to have no end. It seemed to go on for ever. Tremendously long bar. Along the other wall, sort of circular alcoves. Full of smoke, and an odd yellow light. It was like going back a hundred years. Even the people didn't seem quite real. Not that I took in a lot. We just wanted a quiet drink. There was a wine parlour behind the staircase. As we entered, I noticed three girls at a table. Bit tiddly they were; but not too tiddly to giggle as I went past. Had they never seen a chap in a bowler before. What an odd lot they are. Anyway, we got seats and the time passed pleasantly enough. It was nearly ten when I remembered the luggage. We went out, crossed the road to the station. And that's when things started to go wrong. The Left Luggage was closed. I read the notice again. Absolutely no possibility of a mistake. Open till ten. We went straight over to the ticket counter. Hell of a queue there, and time was getting on. My turn finally came. I asked the chappie how I could get my case. Now I will say this, *he* was pleasant enough. He directed us across the platform. We were to ask for some man who was supposed to look after such things. I spoke to the ticket-collector, explained what I wanted. He listened to what I said, pulled from his waistcoat pocket an enormous watch which he proceeded to examine with great solemnity.

He looked up at me:

'Well . . . it's a bad time. No getting round that. One fellow going off, the other due on any minute. You might just catch the one going off.'

'And where would I be likely to find him?' I enquired.

'Up the end, through the barrier and into the office. Any-body'll tell you.'

We found the office. Absolute hive of inactivity. Never seen so many chaps rushing round doing nothing. Least that's what it looked like. I enquired again. They said I was too late for the one, and still too early for the other . . . if he came at all . . . he hadn't been too well! Fellow behind the grille said I'd better go and have a word with yet another official in the station-master's office. He pointed in the direction we'd come. We'd gone right round in a circle, though we were now inside the barrier. There we stood for a few minutes till a smallish chap came out. I addressed him. Right first time. And a right one, too, I can tell you. Had a certain amount of difficulty understanding what he said. That didn't seem to please him either, but they do talk in the most extraordinary way up there.

'You realise it's not my job,' was his reaction, after I had patiently, and politely, for the umpteenth time explained exactly what the problem was.

'You'll have to wait' he said. 'I've got other things to do first.'

Yes, but! . . . I protested. Fat lot of good that was.

He was already half-way across the platform. He shot into a doorway. We walked over to the ticket-collector again and asked if anyone else had a key to the Left Luggage. He told us we'd just have to wait. So there we stood, fuming. On the other side of the barrier, a policeman was chatting to a couple of porters. God, never felt such a fool in all my life. D'you know, he must have realised what was happening, must have heard every word. Do you think he made the slightest attempt to help. On the contrary. At one stage I caught him staring at me. If looks could have killed. Murder on the spot, I can tell you. Couldn't for the life of me think why.

Then it hit me. Jean! He must have thought I was off on a dirty weekend, or something. The very idea! Was I boiling.

Anyway, to cut a long story short, that fellow eventually returned . . . about three-quarters of an hour later. Only a little chap he was, too. Talk about touchy.

'You realise' was his opening remark, 'if I wanted, I could keep you waiting till tomorrow morning.'

'Whatever for?' I managed to get in.

'And,' he continued, 'you can complain to the station-master. I don't care!'

What could you say to a remark like that. I ask you. Though Jean did try. She certainly tried. You know, some-how I don't think he liked me. Or I'd upset him. . . . Who knows? I just wanted my luggage and to get away from him. I'd just about had enough. You never get anywhere with that type, do you?

Another beer? . . . That reminds me, we still had some time to wait before the train went. I didn't want to stick around that station one moment longer, I can tell you. Sud-denly I realised it was long after closing time. What were we to do? Nothing open, apart from a few fish and chip shops. But there's a big hotel right beside the station. I had an idea. We slipped into the hotel bar and I got Jean seated in the corner. Fortunately the bar was still fairly crowded. I waited my turn.

'Yes, sir?' the barman said. I ordered, looking straight at him. He poured the drinks, paused suddenly.

'You are resident, sir?'

'As a matter of fact, I'm not,' I said, continuing to look at him. I slid a pound across the bar.

'Thank you, sir' the barman said. He turned away to serve somebody else.

'I can tell you, I enjoyed that drink. I really did.'

Indian Summer

The sun stopped shining as the train entered the station. Doors opened all down the train; people surged out on to the platform. It took several minutes for the crowd to clear. One of the passengers was left standing as the train drew away. He waited, looked up and down the platform several times before he too set off in the direction of the station exit. Suddenly he saw the girl, outside the barrier, waving excitedly. He raised his hand, waved back.

'You came, you came!' the girl cried. She put her arms around the man's neck, hugged him. He smiled.

'Well, I said I would, didn't I?'

'Yes, but why didn't you write?'

'Didn't you get my letter?'

'Of course not, silly, or I wouldn't have asked.'

'No, I suppose not. But how did you know I'd be on this train?'

'I didn't. I just hoped. It's the last one.'

'Do you mean you've been here since early this morning?'

'It doesn't matter. You came.'

'Well, I promised.'

'I know, but I still can't quite believe it.'

'Perhaps you will in the course of the day.'

'Perhaps I will.'

They walked out of the station into the heat of the sun.

'Your head's shining nicely today,' the girl said.

'My God, what a thing to say to a man who's come hundreds of miles just to see you.'

'You know I didn't mean it. You're not angry are you?'

'Of course not.'

'I didn't think so. Any trouble getting away?'

'No, none at all. . . . I'm often away.'

'What shall we do? It's your day.'

'I'm quite happy walking for the moment. Is it far to your place?'

'We can do it in half an hour. Unless that's going to be too much for you.'

'Now don't start that again.'

'I wasn't. I was being quite serious. You know what you said. . . .'

'It's perfectly all right. I'm enjoying the walk.'

'How long can you stay?'

'I'm not quite sure. I'll have to phone later.'

'Yes, I understand.'

They walked on together, she taking quick strides, almost pulling him along, he more slowly. A woman passed, gave him a look.

'Old bitch!' he said.

'Who?'

'That woman.'

'Don't take any notice. She's probably nuts.'

'Looked more as if she thought you were.'

'Nuts?'

'No, not nuts.'

'Tell you what, we can take a short-cut through the park. It's nice in the park. I often slip over for an hour or so.'

'Yes, I'd like that.'

She took his arm as they went through the main gate.

'Where do you normally go?'

'I'll show you. It's over there by the bowling green. There's hardly ever anyone around during the day.'

They made their way across the park, passed through a gap in the surrounding box hedge. After the long summer the close-cut lawns had a slightly faded look. There was nobody playing on the greens. They sat down on one of the benches, alone except for a young man seated opposite them. He had taken his shirt off. He lay back in the seat, eyes closed, the sun gleaming on his lean muscled body. Neither of them spoke for a few moments. The girl turned to look at the man.

'It doesn't seem possible, does it?'

'What?'

'That summer's nearly over.'

'No sign of it at the moment.'

'No, but I'm back here now.'

'Well, you've got an awful lot ahead of you this year.'

'I know, but I can't even start to think about it at the moment.'

'I suppose not, but you'll have to soon.'

'I know. I expect I'll enjoy it once term has started.'

They got up, walked on through the park. There were only a few people about: several old men, elderly women with small dogs, two boys lying on the grass.

'Not far now,' the girl said after they had walked for some minutes. They aproached a series of low semi-circular blocks with flat roofs. The windows were small, almost slits in the mottled red brick of the walls.

'It's up here,' the girl continued, 'five rooms to a unit. We share kitchen and bathroom. But most people are still on holiday. I'm the only one back at the moment.'

The man followed up the stairs, through the door at the top which she had opened.

'Look!' she said, 'Your letter.'

'Here, let me rip it up. It's no use now,' the man said.

'No, I want it!' the girl said, snatching it up. 'Come on, my room's at the end.'

He entered the room. On the walls, coloured posters of continental places, two empty chianti bottles on a string. A desk by the window, two chairs, bookshelves, and a divan by the wall made the room seem even smaller than it was. A thin gleam of brightness on the bare floor came through from the narrow window. A large woolly bear lay at the head of the bed. The man walked over to the desk, picked up a framed photograph.

'Is that your friend?'

'Yes.'

'He looks very nice.'

'He is.'

'Where is he?'

'He's around.'

'Won't he be coming in to see you?'

'I asked him not to.'

'Won't he be upset?'

'Yes. I don't think he understands anything at the moment. But for goodness sake sit down.'

'Sorry, I was thinking.'

'Oh, you're always thinking.'

The man sat down on the narrow bed, leant back against the wall. The girl came over. They were silent again. It was very quiet in the room. The sound of traffic on the street hardly reached them. The man put his arm along the girl's shoulders, drawing her towards him. The girl let her head rest against his.

'Are you glad you came?' she murmured.

She turned her face to his, kissed him. He breathed in her freshness. Her arms tightened round his neck, pulling him down. They kissed again. He opened his eyes, looked at her. There was colour in her cheeks, tiny drops of moisture on the skin above her lips. She drew him to her again. He felt her body hard against his. He let his hand pass down the girl's body, under the blouse. Her breast rose, swelled under his hand. Her warmth became a part of him as the girl pressed against him. Slowly he took his hand away. The girl was very still. He took her arms, released himself from their hold, sat up on the bed. The girl remained where she was, curled up, the long hair hiding most of her face.

The man got up, walked over to the window.

'Is there a telephone near here?'

'Just up the road.' the girl said. She rolled over on her back, lay staring up at the ceiling.

'You'll be going back this evening?'

'Yes.'

'There's a train in about an hour.'

'That would suit me fine.'

'Will you write?'

'Of course.'

'Are you angry?'

'No.'

'Sorry you came?'

'I. . . .'

'Don't say anything.'

'All right.'

'Don't come near me. Would you draw the curtains.'

'Of course.'

He shut the door quietly behind him, went down the steps again. He could see the telephone kiosk further up the street.

Backward Looks

It wasn't until much later that I noticed his hands. Not that there was anything so very unusual about them. They were very ordinary hands which no doubt plenty of people would have been pleased to find at the end of their sleeves. For a long time I never really registered the fact that Henry had hands at all. But then why should I have? I am not in the habit of studying other people's hands. Yet now that I stop to reflect, I have to admit that even though Henry was such an unforgettable part of those years, I find it difficult to see him clearly. He was substantial enough, in the sense that he had a name, was identifiable: he was certainly no ghost. One was always bumping into him. Yet he was not a person one could easily place or come close to. The more I think of him, the more just passing glimpses come, and go: a remembered look from those pale eyes – were they blue or grey? – a smile just starting, sentences which began with great promise. He was rather good-looking. Tall, though not intimidatingly so. He always seemed to be bending forward slightly, almost deferentially, as if he couldn't bear to miss a single syllable of what one was saying. As I try to re-compose him in my mind's eye I see him standing, walking; never sitting. Why, I wonder. Of course we met mostly at a club, up at the bar. Or I saw him in the street, going about his business. He dressed carefully; neither in nor out of fashion. Something slightly unusual, or a touch of formality – he often wore a flower in his buttonhole – gave him almost the air of a dandy. How strange that such an old-fashioned word should come to mind. Dandy. It's the wrong word, but it's as near as I can get to the impression he left.

He was a friendly, comforting sight. He made you feel he was interested. He was interested. He would always ask questions. Ordinary, expected questions. Gently. The expression on his face intimating concern, but certainly no idle curiosity. His pale eyes regarded you while you spoke, perhaps warming slightly. Perhaps. Or just resting on you, not putting you under any constraint. Discreet eyes; eyes which knew what was expected of them, eyes which were never difficult to look into. I don't think I can have been mistaken. Several of the girls said exactly the same.

How old was he then? Another blank. I think – although I am not sure – we must have been almost the same age. I really don't know. When I was with him I felt he was slightly older, although I couldn't say why. When I saw him with older people he looked very young. Perhaps he had the secret of eternal youth. Certainly in the years I knew him there was no evidence of any outward change.

'Hello, I'm Henry.' Those first words addressed to me I remember with great clarity. I had been going to a quiet little place quite regularly, had seen Henry – or rather, noticed him since I didn't know him yet – but had not spoken to him. He put his hand out, shook mine. A firm, friendly, completely uncompromising act. I wasn't even surprised. Henry was not a man to take one openly by surprise. With him this approach – if approach it was – though unexpected did not seem at all unnatural.

'I'm Henry', he said, as if that was enough, as if the name implied a guarantee of personal soundness, left behind echoes of something slightly grand. I never did find out what his surname was. Or perhaps I did. I'm sure it wouldn't have mattered. At the places where we met mention of Henry's name was enough. Had anybody enquired after Henry and used a surname I am convinced this would have raised eyebrows. It would have bordered on sacrilege.

Henry's unstudied manner – if it was unstudied – was masterly. Though don't ask me to explain how he did it. I

can merely talk about the effect. Henry was always . . . well
. . . Henry.

We talked. Or rather, I talked while Henry listened. I had
not been long in the city, my experiences were still very new.
Henry let all my enthusiasm, confidences, lap over him, not
once by even a flicker of those steady eyes revealing the
slightest suspicion of boredom – although I must have been
extremely boring. He listened, seemed totally absorbed in
my concerns. Effortlessly he let himself into my little world,
permitting me to give him details of my most intimate
thoughts. Even afterwards, when I thought about that meeting, I wasn't upset. Somehow you never minded telling
Henry anything. You never felt for a moment that Henry
would dream of taking advantage of anything embarrassing
or personal which might have slipped out. I enjoyed myself
enormously. I didn't know many people at the time, Henry
was the first person to whom I had talked about my new life.
I felt we had really got to know each other. I felt all the
better for having been with him. He was so very pleasant to
be with. He had such a gentle way of leading one on, of
letting one say what he wanted to hear.

No doubt his voice contributed to this impression, the way
he said things. He chose his words well, never saying much,
somehow building bridges into his sentences which it was so
easy to step on to, and cross.

I do not think he had a particular accent. Certainly no
recognisable touches of dialect, no affectation, even if there
were occasional, not lapses, but expressions which seemed
slightly – ever so slightly – out of place. Again I find the
word 'old-fashioned' coming to mind. Perhaps that's what it
was. But such expressions merely added to the sympathy, or
sympathetic feelings, which he provoked. Even the sound of
his voice was strangely reassuring; his voice an instrument on
which he could convey the subtlest of emotional tones.

I walked back to the office after meeting him that first time.
On the way I suddenly realised that I had not asked him anything about himself, that I had talked uninterruptedly about
myself. As I've said, I was not upset about what I'd revealed

to Henry of myself, but about the fact that I had spoken exclusively about my own personal affairs, and person.

I met Henry some days later, apologised for having been such a bore. He turned slowly to face me, looked straight at me: 'But my dear old chap, it was fascinating, took me right back to my own early days in the city.'

'Do tell me.' I said, wanting to give him an opening.

'Oh, another time. But what have you been doing since we last met?'

That was Henry all over. Neatly turning the conversation away from himself. However I was not to be put off that easily. I asked him what he was up to in the city.

'What everybody else is up to . . . money-grubbing, money-grubbing. Fearfully dull.'

In a tone of voice which implied that further questions would be a breach of good taste. We turned to other subjects, on which I was encouraged to give an opinion. And yet in spite of Henry's professed or intimated dislike of money our conversations nearly always returned to that very topic. Henry would hesitantly refer to ways in which money could be made. Never in such terms as to lead one to suspect he was at all personally involved, but on the other hand never so impersonally as to suggest that the matter was one of total indifference to him. His command, or apparent command, of all the tricks – not a word he would have used – then current was impressive.

He would talk vaguely of things one could do. Not exactly flutters, but short-term stakes, splendid options; little phrases tucked away in other-sounding sentences. Slight emphases, tiny pauses. Occasionally he would make a movement with his hand in the direction of the small black briefcase he invariably had with him. No more than that. I never saw him open it. I somehow got the impression that inside that brief-case were details of financial coups just waiting for the magic moment. For some strange reason I never reacted to Henry's unspoken offers. For offers they most certainly were, even if Henry was never undiplomatic enough to suggest we work together, or that he be my agent on some deal he had in mind.

At the time, with my habits and interests, I could have done with considerably more money than I had.

I said nothing, did nothing. Our conversation would take a less serious turn – after all we were both young – and Henry left me in peace.

In retrospect I suppose I must have sensed that Henry wanted something from me. And yet he couldn't have been nicer about it. Why shouldn't I have listened to his schemes? Plenty of people were making money in those days – big money. Henry never seemed short. Although that is perhaps not quite true now I come to think about it. Although he always appeared to have time on his hands, was seen everywhere, gave the impression of having no financial worries, he did from time to time borrow small sums of money from me. These he invariably did not repay. Since they were small amounts and he was such pleasant company, I didn't bother. Some people are casual about small amounts.

And then he was no longer there. A week, two weeks, several weeks passed. People began to talk. There were rumours of unpaid bills at various drinking places. Some of the girls pulled strange faces when his name was mentioned. There was mention of a wife, possibly more than one, children. But no Henry. I heard, although I do not know if it was true, of enquiries being made on account of dubious stock transactions. I thought of that little black suitcase.

Years passed. I had forgotten all about Henry. Suddenly I saw him, on the other side of the street. I was in a hurry, had just time for a quick glance. No mistake. It was Henry all right. But not quite the same Henry. He was as well-dressed as ever, even still carried a (the?) briefcase. He seemed slightly shrunken, older, his stoop no longer assumed, but real.

That was when I remembered his hands. Funnily enough it was one of the girls who drew my attention to them. It wasn't so much that they were ugly but that one didn't expect Henry's hands to be like that. Trust a girl to notice. It certainly wouldn't have made any difference to me at the time. I liked old Henry, in spite of everything. Everybody did.